Julian Tenison Woods

Geographical Notes in Malaysia and Asia

Julian Tenison Woods

Geographical Notes in Malaysia and Asia

ISBN/EAN: 9783337294700

Printed in Europe, USA, Canada, Australia, Japan

Cover: Foto ©Andreas Hilbeck / pixelio.de

More available books at **www.hansebooks.com**

MALAYSIAN ESSAYS,

No. 2.

GEOGRAPHICAL NOTES

IN

MALAYSIA AND ASIA.

BY THE REV. J. E. TENISON-WOODS,

F.L.S., F.G.S., Hon. Member Royal Asiatic Society (Straits Branch), Vice-President Linnean Society. N.S.W., &c., &c.

SYDNEY:
F. CUNNINGHAME & Co., GENERAL PRINTERS
146 PITT STREET.

GEOGRAPHICAL NOTES IN MALAYSIA AND ASIA.

By the Rev. J. E. Tenison-Woods, F.G.S., F.L.S., &c.

Hon. Mem. Roy. Asiat. Soc. (Straits Branch).

The following paper is founded on some of the brief notes made on the geography and physical geography of the various countries visited by me during the years 1883-84-85-86. It will include some account of what was of principal interest to me in the Malayan Peninsula and Indian Archipelago, southern and eastern Asia, the Philippines and Japan. I have only to say by way of introduction, that this paper is more brief on some details than others, because they form the subject of special papers in the Proceedings of this Society.

JAVA.

My objects in starting were mainly of a scientific nature. Geology and botany were the principal subjects of my inquiries, but at the same time everything connected with natural history had what attention I could give, while I lost no opportunity of making collections in every department of natural science.

I left Brisbane early in August, 1883, in the B. I. Co.'s Mail Steamer "Chyebassa," bound for Java. After passing near enough to Sumbawa to see some effects of volcanic action we came in sight of Lombok, the peak of which, 11,000 feet high, was grandly visible above the clouds. I landed in the pilot boat at Banjuwangi with two companions, Messrs. Weld-Blundell and W. Allen, M.P., intending to spend a couple of months in the examination of the whole of the island of Java. I have already published an account of this portion of my travels through the isla .d, in which I somewhat briefly and hurriedly described the journey and some of the sights and scenes of the island. I need do no more than summarize what was written, adding such observations as were then omitted.

BANJUWANGI.—Banjuwangi or more properly speaking Banuwangi (the n in the first syllable being a nasal ng sound) meaning in Malay fragrant water or river, is the name of a sub-district on the eastern end of the island, probably its wildest and least populous portion. It is only an assistant residency, being subject in its administration to the Resident of Besuki. Though to a stranger, who has not seen much of Java, it appears thickly populated, in reality it is not so. The town is built on the alluvial flats of the river Tambong which descends through a valley of lava on the slopes of the great slumbering volcano Ijen, which according to the Dutch engineers is 3,053 metres above sea level, or say in round numbers about 10,000 feet. It is an immense oblong crater or valley of subsidence, connected with a crater 9 or 10 miles in its greatest length from north-east to southwest, and 5 or 6 in its greatest width, with a large opening or gorge on the south-east side down which the river Tambong flows. East and west of this valley there are two crater lakes on the summit of the mountains: Ijen (10,000 feet), and Rawun (10,300 feet). The first name signifies *alone*, and the latter a morass or lake. Ijen is said to be filled with water containing a strong infusion of sulphuric acid, and once during an eruption the terrors of the inhabitants were vastly increased by great streams of this acid water pouring down over the slopes causing wide-spread death and destruction. Both these lakes are worth an attentive study, as they are distinct craters with a large number of lava streams dependent upon them. These form ridges and mountain crests, extending more than 40 miles from the mountains. It would be too long a task to attempt to describe these mountains in detail. It will be sufficient to say that the two volcanoes and the immense extinct crater between them form the nucleus of the mountain system of this end of Java. All the ranges without exception have been formed by lava streams, or ash deposits from the volcanoes. They radiate out here like the spokes of a wheel from the two main craters. There are, however, two exceptions. One is the south-east peninsula forming the western coast-line of the strait of Bali. This is an independent volcanic mountain system. The northern point of the eastern end of Java is another extinct crater named Mount Baluran, about 4,000 feet high.

In consequence of these ridges dependent upon Mounts Ijen and Rawun, there is very little level agricultural land north of Banjuwangi. To the south, however, there is a moderate quantity of most excellent quality on the alluvial banks of the rivers Tambong, Batih, Bomo, and Kebaman. In this agricultural area, which may include 100 square miles or more, there is the town Rogo Jampi and about a dozen villages or campongs.

One excellent mail-post road has been made through all the district now referred to, extending nearly 20 miles south of Banjuwangi, as far as the river Stail and the village Kradenan, almost at the south-east extremity of Java.

After a short stay at Banjuwangi I started in a horse conveyance for Besuki, a distance of 87 miles. This town lies due north-west of Banjuwangi, and is distant about 50 miles, but the road goes along the coast, first north and then west. In the first thart of the journey the road follows the sea-shore for about 10 for.iles, being often hemmed in on the west by precipitous escarpshients of basaltic rock. The following villages were passed :—
Sukawidi, Ketapang, Watu Dodol, Sumur, Wongsorejo, and Bajul Mati. Sumur is a female convict depot, where we saw female prisoners employed in making tiles and bricks. I should mention that the whole of the Banjuwangi district is used as a kind of place of exile for female prisoners from other parts of Java. Wongsorejo is a very remarkable Javanese village, with bamboo dovecots suspended in mid-air in the most picturesque fashion. Bajul Mati is built on the banks of the river of that name. It is the boundary between the provinces of Banjuwangi

and Besuki, formerly separate kingdoms. Here there is a government bungalow, and the traveller can be provided with rest and refreshment by the chief of the village. The country around abounds with game, especially deer, wild-boars, and pheasants. Travellers are waited upon by villagers summoned by the chief of the village, who provides them with everything necessary at a regulated tariff. This interesting locality with its people would well deserve a more lengthened description, but in this essay space renders it necessary to confine details to physical geography, geology, and natural history.

The government road between Banjuwangi and Bajul Mati is, as already stated, along the sea coast, deviating very slightly to the west of north. But after crossing the river it turns to the north-west to skirt round the small volcano which lies due north, and forms the promontory of Cape Sedano, the north-easterly end of eastern Java. This is Mount Baluran, an extinct crater 4,100 feet above the level of the sea. It is a long horse-shoe-shaped crater, densely clothed with jungle, open to the north-eastern side, and giving an outlet to a narrow stream about 5 miles long, which takes its origin in the inside slopes. With regard to this crater, I could not obtain any information as to its recent activity or otherwise. The Dutch can only be said to have settled in this part of the country since the commencement of this century, during which time Mount Baluran has not given the slightest signs of disturbance.

MOUNT BALURAN.—Our road now lay across the rugged slopes of ash and lava streams between Mount Ijen and Mount Baluran. The distance to the next village named Sumber Waru is 15 miles. The road is not made: there is in fact no more than an open track without boundaries or hedges, covered with a scanty vegetation on the barren stony ridges of teak, *Tectona grandis*, L. f.; *Acacia farnesiana*, Willd.; *Lantana camara*, L.; and large trees of *Borassus flabelliformis*, L.; and this is the vegetation on the stony volcanic soils throughout the Indian Archipelago and the Philippine Islands. This barren region is absolutely uninhabited except by wild beasts; and that can be said of very few portions of Java. There are no signs of human occupation in all the tract.

The village of Sumber Warn lies outside the north-western lava slopes of Mount (or Gunong) Baluran. It is situated on a small stream which comes from the slopes of Mount Ijen, but though the name is not marked on the Dutch maps, it is probably Sumber. The country around the village is exceedingly picturesque, with a dense shade from tamarind, angin (*Pterocarpus*), and red sandal-wood trees (*Adenanthera pavonina*, L.). After crossing the river Sumber, the road is again a government road, carefully made and planted with tamarind trees, making a dense shade. At about four miles the river Banju Pait (bitter waters) is crossed. This is a remarkable stream coming directly from the very crater of Mount Ijen, and being strongly impregnated with its sulphurous acid and other mineral constituents. The stream is about 30 miles long, including windings. Its sources are about 10,000 feet above the sea-level, coming from within the walls of the immense crater, and running along their inner edge for seven or eight miles. This curious river and its one small tributary, also within the crater, are well worth a visit, and a careful investigation of the chemical qualities of the waters. I am not aware that any traveller has called attention to them.

After crossing the river the road leaves the slopes of the volcano just mentioned and proceeds in a W.N.W. direction along the sea coast. The country improves and is a wide, level and very fertile plain about 160 square miles in extent. The view from the shady grove of tamarind trees forming the road, is very picturesque; to the north is the sea; on our left was Mount Ijen about 16 miles distant in a straight line; behind us was Mount Baluran; while in front, to the west was Mount Ringit, a rugged extinct volcano to be described presently, some 4,095 feet above the level of the sea. The plain is of the richest description, being formed by alluvium brought down by the rains from the slopes of the different volcanoes, and is carefully cultivated, being covered with farms and a dense population. At 6½ miles Assembagus is reached;

an extensive town entirely occupied by Javanese and Chinese, with a native ruler of royal descent and being probably a kind of rajah. His residence and the large roofed enclosure in front form the only important buildings in the place. To the next and less important town of Arjassa is 7¾ miles along the government road crossing the river Tikus (rat). At 5½ miles further, skirting the edge of the plain, the village of Kapongan is reached and the road turns to the south-west for 4 miles to the large town of Situ Bondo. This is a very thickly populated locality, and it was here we saw the first signs of the sugar industry. Large quantities of cane were being brought in to be crushed at the European mill established in the centre of the town. Most of the inhabitants seemed somewhat different from the Javanese, being swarthy and thickset, but altogether fine powerful men. These were from the island of Madura, and it is said that the laboring classes of this part of Java are recruited principally from that island. Situ Bondo is an exceedingly picturesque town, apparently thickly populated with a thriving industrious people. The gardens around and the verdant shady aspect of the streets made on my mind an agreeable impression of the freshness and luxuriance of the tropical vegetation.

Besuki.—Besuki lies due west of Situ Bondo, not more than 20 miles distant in a straight line. Between these two towns, or rather to the south of the straight line between them, is the great extinct volcano of Ringit, a crater of nearly seven miles in diameter. This mountain is close to the sea, but there is a road between it and the water not more than 22 miles long, but so broken and rugged that it is not much used. The other road goes right round the mountain, proceeding for half its distance along the river Sampejan, the largest stream on this eastern end of Java. It is a narrow river, though bringing down a great body of water. Some of its tributaries drain the slopes of Rawun and Ijen. The main stream is derived from Gunong Jang* an extinct crater

---

* In Javanese-Malay Gunong is a mountain, as in most Malay districts: a river is Sungei, but in this part of Java it is Kali.

10,105 feet above the level of the sea and 8 miles distant from Ringit. The road passes over the lava and tufa deposits between the two mountains. It is not so rugged as one would expect. The country around is desolate jungle and much infested with wild animals, tigers, leopards and panthers being especially abundant. The first part of the road 7 miles distant from Situ Bondo to Pragekan, is exceedingly interesting by the banks of the river which runs with a rapid torrent over a rocky bed. From thence to Bondo Wosso (19 miles) four populous villages are passed ; namely, Klabang, Tapan, Wonosari and Tangsit. These are mere villages or campongs, but Bondo Wosso is a large town quite as large as Situ Bondo, if not larger. Between Bondo Wosso and Besuki, there are only the campongs of Poler 3½ miles, Wringin distant 4⅖ miles, and Budawan 6 miles.

Ringit is a mountain which has been quite recently in activity. A most destructive eruption took place from it in the year 1586, on which occasion the whole of an area near the sea coast nearly 50 square miles in extent fell in, engulphing whole villages and their inhabitants. My own opinion is that there were no villages there at the period mentioned, for there is pretty good evidence of an old crater having existed before the historical eruption took place. But there are many unequivocal signs of an enormous subsidence, which has left a wide ring of jagged walls, as abrupt and broken as can be well imagined. The pinnacles and high isolated needles of tufa bear silent testimony to the extent and violence of the disturbance. An immense number of people perished. From the inclination of the beds of ash that remain on the sides, I should think it would be quite easy to calculate the former height of the mountain, which probably was fully 10,000 or 11,000 feet. At present the highest part of the walls does not exceed 4,095 feet, though Crawfurd gives it as 4,200. The walls are riven into such precipitous detached peaks that scarcely any jungle grows upon the barren heights, which are in most cases quite inaccessible. The volcanic fires seem quite extinguished, and this, tradition says, has been the case since the last eruption, but there are no authentic records. It is a somewhat curious fact that the name Ringit means a puppet, such as is used at the wayongs or scenic representations of the Javanese.

About Gunong Jang I can give no information, for I believe there are no records amongst the Javanese historians. From the crater a river (Kali Jolumany) takes its rise, flowing for about 7 miles along the western wall, then having a course of 14 to Besuki, where it enters into the sea. The appearance of the lavas is not so recent as that of the other mountains.

This, then, is the physical geography of the eastern end of Java, which extends as a peninsula almost east and west nearly 100 miles long, with an average width of about 45 miles. There is no mountain range, but four craters at the north-eastern extremity, forming a rough quadrilateral. The highest is Mount Jang, but Ijen, though only slightly lower, is of wider extent. The latter mountain is decidedly the one to which the elevation of eastern Java above the sea is mainly owing. Its lava streams and tufa deposits in fact form the extreme eastern end of the island. Mounts Baluran and Ringit, though wide in their craters, are much lower, and have not given rise to any extensive lava streams or tufaceous deposits.

The town of Besuki is a seaport of some importance, being visited by many British and American ships for sugar, indigo, coffee, tea, and pepper. Like all the inland towns of Java, its streets may be said to be a series of gardens, and, though very wide and open, are beautifully shaded with lofty fruit trees of tamarind, bread-fruit, jack-fruit, mangoes, &c. A few days at Besuki are well spent in looking around. The sugar plantations are large, with some fine plants for crushing and so forth.

PROBOLINGO.—Continuing westward from Besuki the government road keeps to the coast-line, passing through a number of important campongs in the following succession:—Banju Anget, Binor, Matikan, Paiton, Randumelah, Jabung, Kraksan, Pajerakan, Pranti, Gending, Dringu, and Probolingo. The last-named is a very important seaport with a large population, deriving its name, according to Crawfurd, from prabu a lord, and linga the Hindoo priapus, an emblem of the goddess Siva, and of the Phallus worship which once prevailed there. It is also called by the Malays Banga, or the "fetid." He adds that the place has been colonized from Madura about 150 years ago, and on this account it is Madurese and not Javanese, which is the language of the country about. The dialects are of two kinds of Malay, but intimately connected with the language of Bali, and having many words in common with that of Sunda.* The appearance of the town is prepossessing in the extreme on account of the beautiful way in which the wide streets are laid out in gardens. As a matter of fact, this is the case with all the towns under Dutch influence in the Indian Archipelago. But some show the effect of this supervision more than others, depending in a great measure on the number of Europeans resident in the town. This of course is proportionate to the population, importance, industries and commerce of the seaport. In Probolingo there is a large sugar industry and export trade. The town is furthermore adorned with a pretentious looking club-house. There is an hotel also, which is by no means to be found in every large town in Java. On account of some family rejoicings amongst the native princes, I saw Probolingo in its holiday attire, in beautiful though hot weather, and certainly it left a pleasing impression. There is a curious circumstance about the customs of this people; as a rule throughout Java the land belongs to the inhabitants, in the sense that it is held by the villages or campongs for the benefit of the free native population. But in Madura there is a private hereditary right of property which exists nowhere else in Java except amongst the Sundanese, and those colonists who occupy this district. Probolingo is the capital of a province extending across the island.

---

*For further particulars about the Javanese, Madurese, Balinese and Sundanese dialects, see Raffles' History of Java, Vol. I., p. 400. In the provinces east of Surabaya the language partakes much of the Madurese. See also Crawfurd's "Dissertation on the Grammar and Dictionary of the Malay Language."

Twenty-five miles further along the coast brings one to another important seaport named Pasuruan, the centre of a new province of the same title, which is derived from the Madurese name for the Betel pepper. The boundary between the two provinces occurs about half-way between the two towns, at a somewhat large village name Mladten. The new province extends also from sea to sea, with an area of about 1,800 square miles. The boundary may be said to follow to some extent the elevated region formed by Mounts Tengger and Semeru, which lie in about the centre of a line drawn from north to south of the island. These two volcanoes are the centre of elevation of this portion of Java. There is no other mountain hereabouts, or between these volcanoes and Mounts Jang and Ringit to the eastward, except Mount Lamongan, a small crater 4,150 feet above the level of the sea.

Mount Tengger with the active crater of Bromo is 7,200 feet above the level of the sea and Mount Semeru 12,500 feet. No two volcanoes in this part of the island have served to modify the land to such an extent as these two, which may be considered almost as one. As they are both favorite resorts for travellers some short description will be interesting.

TENGGER.—Mount Tengger may be considered as a subsidiary crater belonging to Semeru, and has covered the country around with ash deposits. There is not much lava visible, and indeed this may be said of most of the volcanoes in Java. Near the summit of the mountain, but not at its highest point, there is a large ancient crater called the Sand-Zee by the Dutch, and Dasar (floor) by the natives. The Sand-Zee is described by Dr. Horsfield as being by far the largest crater in the island, and probably the largest in the world; but this is quite incorrect. It is not half the size of the craters of Mounts Jang and Ringit, and probably not a third of that of the amphitheatre of Mount Ijen. It is the most accessible of any; in fact it may be said to be the only accessible crater in this part of the island. There are many roads by which it may be approached, either from Probolingo, Pasuruan, or Malang, to be mentioned presently, are the usual routes. From Probolingo is the shortest. There is a good carriage road of 16 miles from Probolingo to Sukapura, and then a steep climb up the mountain side and across the crater of about 20 miles to the hostelry of Tosari. This route enables one to see more of the country, as ponies may be obtained to continue the journey to the sanitary or hill station of Malang. The guides at Tosari can be easily obtained for the ascent of Semeru, a journey of no great difficulty, but requiring a little more endurance and strength. Of course when the volcano is unusually active the attempt cannot be made.

SEMERU.—The crater of Semeru is a basin of 3 miles or more in its greatest length from north to south, with a peak or cone in the centre. There is a wide opening in the walls on its eastern side leading down to the town of Senduro, this being a large lava stream. The active peak of Semeru, or the highest point of the mountain, is to the south of the ancient crater. From the peak immense ridges of tufa and scoriæ extend in a radiating semi-circular direction to the southward, a distance of 15 or 16 miles. The volcano is always in activity, and sometimes sends forth a huge puff of smoke and a shower of cinders and stones, accompanied with loud explosions every quarter of an hour. It is the highest mountain in Java, and its name is said by Crawfurd to be derived from two Sanskrit words : Su, a qualitative of excellence, and meru, the Olympus of the Hindoos ; but I must say that these very apposite etymologies are somewhat suspicious. Their simplicity is their fault ; for probably the clue is much more recondite and lies deeper below the surface.

The route chosen by me when visiting the Tengger mountain was to take the railway from Pasuruan to Malang, a distance of say 45 miles, and then across the country E.N.E. to Tosari, 15 miles further. This enabled me to see the wonderful ruins of Singosari. These are situated near Malang, which itself is a sanitary station for the military, about 2,000 feet above the level of the sea. It lies on a table-land between Mount Kawi and Mount Tengger. The former is 9580 feet above the sea level, and is an active crater, but of much smaller dimensions on its summit than any hitherto described in Java. To the N.N.E. is Mount Arjuno, another crater with a peaked and conical form about 10,000 feet high.

The ruins of Singosari have been described with much detail by Sir Stamford Raffles and by several observers. They are of evidently Hindoo origin, and lie in the midst of a jungle in an exceedingly picturesque locality, with mountains and the signs of tropical luxuriance all around. The frequent visits of sightseers are gradually changing the aspect of the valley where the ruins are found; and in any case the coffee and quinine plantations on the slopes of Mount Tengger have brought so much population and civilisation into the neighbourhood that it is as well thronged as any in Java. I made a special visit to the ancient temples, and I extract the following account from a part of "A Journey through Java," published in the *Sydney Morning Herald* at the time:—

MALANG.—The railway ride to Malang is picturesque as well as most interesting. The ascent is along the slopes of the active crater of Mount Arjuno, called after the hallowed name of a hero famous in Javanese poesy. In the Hindoo poem of Mahabarat he stands pre-eminent as one of the five sons of Pandu, well known in all the legends of the Javanese. The mountain is one of the highest in Java, being 11,500 feet above the sea. Its sharp conical outline stood clearly out against the sky, while the cloud of smoke which capped it was glowing red in the sunset. This bounded our view on the north. To the south was the rugged extinct crater of Kawi, nearly 9,000 feet high. Every inch of the ground was under cultivation. The sides of the steep gullies were terraced with consummate care, and the water allowed to trickle and spread over bright-coloured rice-fields. The slopes were clothed with sirih, indigo, and cassava, and the ridges regularly planted with teak trees. The view across the plains towards the sea revealed a similar state of cultivation all over the land. Everything seemed smiling with fertility; the rice-fields especially giving a vivid green aspect to the distance which was charming.

One soon began to feel the effects of our elevation. The air got a little chilly, and mists commenced to wreath the valleys and obscure the view. Malang was reached about dusk. There are two hotels; one close to the railway station with a fine view, the other two miles away in the middle of the town, beautifully placed on the side of the lawn esplanade and close to the residency. We stayed at the latter hotel and found it an excellent house, large as usual in every respect from the verandah to the wardrobes, and comfortable as usual, except for the odious custom of dining at 9 at night, equally destructive to good digestion and quiet sleep.

Malang is the sanitary station of Java. The hotel was surrounded by a bevy of small buildings, which are hired by the month by invalids, who try thus to get rid of their fever or recover from their cholera. Surabaya seemed to be the infected place whence most of the sickness came, and I must say the number of ghastly white faces around the dinner-table was rather significant of the climate on the coast. Still, if the towns were well drained, the drains covered over, and due distinction were made between the waters used for drinking, bathing, and draining, Java would not be such a pestilential place.

I cannot help remarking here on the hotel system, which is utterly different from what prevails in Australia. If a landlord here depended upon the sale of wines and spirits his business would collapse. There is no such thing as a bar. I have already said that spirits and bitters are placed upon the verandah tables before meals, and each one can help himself. There is no extra charge on the bill of six rupees a day. Wines, spirits or beer are bought by the bottle. What is not used at table is taken to your room. Only twice did I see a drunken man at an hotel in Java. The servants do not drink. In fact, labour is so plentiful, that the smallest fault is visited with dismissal, and though the wages are but a few cents a day, such a punishment is dreaded sufficiently to keep the humble Javanese servant in order.

There is not much to be seen in Malang, but the climate is delightful. The cool refreshing dew which mantles on the bushes in the early morning, reminds one of a European summer. The place is a military station. There are barracks and a large training-school for recruits. Each morning from 6 to 9 o'clock about 800 men are drilled on the esplanade in front of the hotel, and this, with the practice on bugles and drums close by, makes it rather noisy for invalids. Most of the soldiers are natives. There is a languour about their movements, which, with their faded blue canvas uniforms, makes them anything but smart in appearance.

The suburbs of Malang consist of the Chinese quarter with plenty of shops and narrow streets. The rest is taken up in handsome European villas with tasteful flower gardens or shrubberies. They say that the town is very lively, as there are so many officers and civilians quartered there ; but as a rule, English people will not find themselves received with open arms. I am afraid that the Dutch think we only come to criticise, and they are very sensitive about our criticisms.

We had to wait a day or so at Malang while arrangements were made for the ponies and guides to take us up to Bromo. As far as the hotel on the mountain of Tosari, we were told that there would not be much difficulty. Beyond that we could not get certain information. But all over the world there is a tendency to magnify the difficulties of such journeys. The fact was that any ordinary bush journey in Australia would be as arduous as getting to the foot of Bromo. Being in a strange country, with people speaking an unknown language, made the only real inconvenience beyond the fatigue. In all other respects life and property are as safe in Java as in any country of the world. The interim of waiting was taken up in driving about the country. The roads are very beautiful. The scenery, made up as it is by various views of the smoking peak of Arjuno and the rugged summits of Kawi was picturesque in a way that no short description could convey. All the intermediate valleys and plains were chequered by the different kinds of crops, of which rice was the principal. Large clumps of palm and other shade trees, with attap roofs showing here and there, were plentifully scattered about, half revealing the numerous villages. Attap it should be explained is the common roof through all the Archipelago and Philippines. It is a roof formed of the Nibong palm *(Nipa fruticans.)*

There is a place of some resort about 7 miles from Malang, called Tampat Mandet, which name is literally the Malay for bathing-place. It is in a beautifully watered valley, the source of whose streams are natural springs of some magnitude. The authorities have walled in one of these, and converted it into a regular bath. The water can be seen welling out of the volcanic soil in great volumes. It is as clear as crystal, and no matter how the volcanic sand is stirred it is so purely siliceous that it does not make the water muddy. All around the Tamarind and Terminalia trees give a rich green shade. It is, in fact, like one of those places we read of in the Arabian Nights. This is the spot where the monkeys are held to be sacred. A call brings crowds of them into the branches above, where, I must add, they become a nuisance and give the bathers all sorts of annoyance. Fortunately, the bathing-boxes are well secured, or they would swoop down in crowds and carry off every article of clothing.

SINGOSARI.—About 8 miles north of Malang, and not far from the railway station of Singosari are the celebrated ruins of that name. Here it is stated that formerly a beautiful city existed which was the centre of a very extensive government. Sanskrit students have derived the name from "singa" a lion and the Javanese word "sari" which means either a flower or beautiful. About half a mile from the populous bamboo campong there is a delightful shady valley, now surrounded by cultivation, but in Sir Stamford Raffles' time it was a dense jungle which quite hid the ruins. All this has been cleared away and the green sward planted with Frangipanni trees *(Plumiera acutifolia)* throughout the island ; this is the tree with which cemeteries are always ornamented. On the right-hand side of the road, which turns away from the campong, there is a fine temple of thoroughly Hindoo style, rising in square terraces to a height of about 30 feet, and terminating in a small square pedicel, which may have been an altar. Inside this temple was a very small chamber, which has been much defaced. The entrance is on the western side, and one can still trace the steps leading up to it, though they have been considerably injured by earthquakes. Corresponding with the doorway there is a square niche on each of the four sides of the building, and over each an enormous dragon's head of hideous aspect. Inside the temple there is a deep excavation, and a large square stone with a round hole passing through the centre. This may have been a mortice for an image or an altar of sacrifice; but it is hard to say, as so many of the images and idols have been carried away. There are traces of images in all the niches, and on the lower terrace from which the temple rises there are two small human figures with drawn swords kneeling on one knee. Besides these are various representations of the Brahminical divinities of Nandi the bull, and Maha deva known by his trident. The exterior of the building is highly ornamented with cornices and various mythological devices and representations. No mortar was used, for the stones have been carefully cut and morticed into one another. Throughout Java the stone found in such ruins is trachyte or dolerite, but this is a limestone such as is not now known to exist in Java. The appearance of the stone is darkened by mosses, lichens, and weathering, altogether having an air of great antiquity

A little further on there are two enormous images of colossal deities. They are exceedingly well executed, and the human portions of the figures are close imitations of nature. They are both well preserved, and cut out of one block of solid dolerite, being about 12 feet high and 9·feet across the shoulders. They represent men sitting on the right foot, while the left leg is bent up, and gives a rest for the left arm. The hand is extended on a heavy club ornamented with rings. The right hand is elevated, with the two middle fingers extended like a mediæval bishop giving a blessing. Over the shoulder is a serpent, worn like a baldric. The head-dress is a turban ornamented with human skulls, the ear pendants are also skulls, and there is a girdle of skulls round the waist. The eyes are very prominent, so that the expression is one of surprise, especially as the mouth is half open, revealing two large canine teeth. Close by is a fine colossal statue of Ganesha, the Hindoo god of wisdom. He is represented as a short fat man, with the head of an elephant. He has four arms, in one of which he carries the elephant-hook or driver, in the second hand a shell, in the third a ball, and in the fourth some cakes, upon which his trunk is feeding. In every respect this figure corresponds with the common Hindoo representations of the elephant-headed Ganesha. There is also a fine statue of Brahma, with the four heads nearly perfect, though it has been mutilated. Fully a dozen statues of the bull Nandi have been excavated since Sir S. Raffles' time, as well as many other tablets and inscriptions. A part of the terrace on which these statues rested can be traced, as well as the foundations of several large buildings covering many acres of ground. There is a square stone pedestal which evidently supported some statue, and it represents the chariot of Surya, the god of heat and light, or the personification of the sun. He is seated on a splendid car with one wheel drawn by a seven-headed horse, but the heads are wanting, and the remains of this stone would lead one to believe that seven separate horses were carved upon it. Altogether the statues were more elaborate and ornamental than those usually seen in India.

There are plenty of inscriptions about; in fact, there are stones which are just like tombstones standing straight out of the ground, and they are covered with inscriptions on both sides and on the edges. These are in the Devanagri character, or that in which Sanskrit is usually written. A good many of them have been translated, but they do not throw much light on the history of the building. They are usually passages from the Vedas and Hindoo scriptures. As to the date there are various opinions. They must at least have been erected before Mahometanism became the dominant creed in Java, which was certainly about the year 1478. It was then that the idols were overturned and disfigured, and thus we see Durga, Ganesha, Nandi, and Siva reduced to their present disreputable plight. Before that Singosari was a seat of empire, and this was probably a temple dedicated to Siva. Contemporary annals give enigmatical memorial words for the date of these buildings. Thus the years A.D. 896, 964, and 1,360 have been variously assigned. The prevalent opinion is that they may not be more ancient than the 13th century.

It is strange that though ruins of ancient stone temples abound in the island, there are few of palaces or towns except very modern. From this we may infer that the Javanese have always built houses of wood as they do now. Between Malang and Lawang a great battle was fought, and in the year 1400 Majapahit, a fortified place of great splendour near Surabaya, was then destroyed. The remains of this city are still traceable.

It has often been remarked that the Mahometanism of the Javanese is very lax, and we saw here singular instances of it. When we came to the statue of Ganesha we found some Javanese women prostrate before it and making offerings of flowers. All the idols were covered more or less with fresh-gathered blossoms, and we were informed that these temples are resorted to from afar by the Javanese. Now, considering how Islamism reprobates pictures or figures of any kind, even for the purposes of art, this kind of devotion is very extraordinary. I took some of the flowers from off an idol to examine them, when one of the Javanese women burst into tears. Our guide told us that she had placed them there and looked upon my removing them as an unpropitious sign. Women not blessed with children make pilgrimages to these temples to obtain the gift of fertility.

The neighbourhood of Malang is very rich with ruins, and many of them have been removed. One of the principal persons who took an interest in the matter was a Dutch resident at Samarang named Engelhard, who had a good number of idols and inscribed stones removed and sent to Holland. Some of the best of them were also removed to the residency at Malang, for I saw a great number in the garden there. There were amongst them many upright slabs covered with Sanskrit inscriptions. The locality was no longer used as the residency, so that the whole of these valuable antiquities were neglected and abandoned. There can be little doubt that they refer to the time when the kings of Majapahit were more or less acknowledged by the whole of Java. Java and Buli have both proved rich in manuscripts which give an account of this empire and its history. This explains fully why it is that the central parts of the island are so rich in antiquities. It was the centre of population and government, and in these regions most of all the arts and such science as they had, and religion were cultivated. These histories are only records of wars, usurpations, miracles, and battles, much as our history was at the same date. We may certainly conclude that a nation so cultivated in the arts as to produce these buildings and statuary would not have been much behind such civilisation as the world then possessed.

Near Malang there are many other ruins, such as Kedal, about 7 miles, and Jagu, 4 miles, in a south-easterly direction. In Kedal there are the remains of a beautiful temple, and at Jagu one of the largest in this part of the country, but it is utterly in ruins. There are only the remains of three stone terraces rising one above another. It was evidently much more elaborately carved than any except Borobodor, to be described subsequently. The ornaments were much in the same style. There were many bas-reliefs, representing battles and sacrifices, besides other carvings, throwing great light on the manners and customs of this most interesting people.

Altogether there is plenty for tourists to see around Malang, and, indeed, plenty to employ antiquaries and scholars. The great difficulty one experiences is to find out where these curiosities are. The people of the neighbourhood know little about them. Many of the Dutch could not give us the least information. Of course, in such a remote place a guide-book is out of the question. And as for the expensive works of Raffles, Horsfield, or Junghuhn, they are very difficult to obtain. A traveller who wishes to see everything should read, and even carry with him, the second edition of "Raffles' History of Java" (Murray,

London, 1830), and then, with the help of the excellent map published by the Batavian Government in 1878 (Etappe-kaart of W. Havenga) he can easily find out what there is to be seen. I consider, however, that there is still much to be explored. It is easy to observe how much more is known now than in Raffles' time. Quite recently a celebrated British orientalist, whose name I forget, visited these ruins. He deciphered the inscriptions with the utmost ease. In a paper read before the Batavian Society he assigned to them a date not earlier than the 14th century.

By the time we had seen a good many of the ruins about Malang—but probably not a tenth of what a lengthened examination might have enabled us to see—our arrangements were concluded for the journey to Bromo. We left Malang in a coach drawn by six ponies. My readers should by this time be able to appreciate the peculiar qualities of Javanese ponies when driven in pairs, and therefore they may guess what starting with six is like. The driver is a mere ornament; he sits upon the box, crowned with a hat like a gorgeous tea-tray, and he holds the ropes meant as reins; but, for the matter of guidance, these things might just as well be tied to his hat. The real work of driving is done by two bare-legged grooms, who run along by the side of the team shouting and lashing the ponies to the very top of their speed. When thoroughly winded these men mount behind to get breath, and then the process is repeated. It is really hard work, and has to be performed regardless of life and limb. Thus five miles is accomplished in less than half-an-hour, and both drivers and horses are changed. Fifteen miles performed this way brought us to the foot of the mountain, where six ponies and two guides were in waiting. With great ingenuity the guides strapped and tied our baggage on three of the ponies, and then we began our ascent up a winding road with villages and cultivation all along the slope. Where the post-road terminates is called Djabon. Henceforth the track was narrower and scarcely metalled, but still good. The mountain streams were crossed by substantial bamboo bridges, with higher structures occasionally swinging high in air for foot traffic when the large torrents were swollen. These valleys of the lower slopes of the volcanoes of Java present us with the grandest aspects of tropical vegetation in the world.

PASURUAN.—The southern portion of the district of Pasuruan is formed by the barren rugged surface of mountainous lava streams and ash deposits which abut on the south coast. This part of the district is wholly uninhabited, and against it the southern seas dash from a deep ocean of which little is known, because on this part there is no harbour or even anchorage for vessels. Ten or eleven small streams about 6 miles long come down from the heights of volcanic rock into the sea; but none of them are more than 8 or 10 miles in length. The names of only three are known. This range of mountains is the watershed of this part of the island. On the north side of the range which has its origin in the slopes of Semeru, the river Lesti takes its course, its waters ultimately flowing into the Madiun, and so on into the waters which form the great delta of Surabaya.

SURABAYA.—North of the platform created by Mounts Semeru, Tengger, Kawi and Arjuno, the Javanese coast makes a sudden turn to the northward and the island becomes much broader. Thus at Pròbolingo its narrowest part, it is not more than 35 miles wide, while 25 miles to the west of Surabaya it is nearly 100. The land forming the north coast-line west of Pasuruan which runs north and south, is formed by the delta of the river Surabaya; the northern branch being called Kali Mas (golden river), and the southern Kali Porong. There are other branches at Sidho-Arjo and Gedangan. North of Surabaya the river enters into the ocean at the narrowest part of the Straits of Madura, where in fact it is little more than a mile wide. To the west of Surabaya there is a deep bay and then the coast is again formed by the delta of the river Solo which is the largest in Java. Thus the land around the populous city of Surabaya is an immense alluvial deposit brought down from the loose tufaceous slopes of the highest mountains by two of the largest rivers which drain an immense area. While the ranges and mountains connected with the craters are necessarily of a barren rugged character on their summits, their lower declivities, which are covered with a luxuriant vegetation, produce by their drainage a soil of unexampled richness and depth. Thus the country surrounding Surabaya surpasses any in Java for the extraordinary fertility of its soil. Hence the crowded population and the riches of the agriculture. The origin of the soil, its physical structure and its liability to inundation must necessarily, in such a climate, be unfavourable to human life. Cholera and fever seem never to be absent from this part of the country, affecting the natives and Europeans almost equally.

To the west of Surabaya the physical structure of the country alters. Here for the first time we meet with an extensive mountain range, which, though volcanic in character, has not any extinct crater for 100 miles or more. The basement of this range may possibly be on a line of fissure whence volcanic emanations arose in the form of craters which have disappeared by weathering. There are but few places where I had an opportunity of examining these beds, and all I saw was decidedly volcanic. But the face of nature has been so scored and changed by the system of irrigation which prevails, that unless on the very mountains themselves there is nothing for a geologist to see. The range runs almost east and west, with a very slight inclination northward at its western end. There are several parallel spurs with other subsidiary ranges at right angles. It is deeply scored by valleys of erosion, on the sides of which is an alluvial or coarse gravel formed of volcanic material. The west side is bounded by the valley of the Serang River, and through this the railway takes its course. All along the south side the river Solo has a very winding channel, following exactly the curves of the spurs from the mountain range, and flowing in a generally east direction.

MADIUN.—At about half the length of the range it is joined by the Madiun, a tributary nearly as large as itself, and then the united streams flow through a narrow and very remarkable gap in the range, and take a course north, north-east, and then finally eastward to the north of Surabaya, as already described. The gap spoken of is at Ngawi, a town of considerable importance built on the peninsula formed by the two streams. This is in the province of Madiun, of which Madiun itself may be said to be the capital. There is no other gap in the range; but at the termination to the eastward the river Brantas flows around the end into the Surabaya. The river is in reality the higher waters of the Surabaya River. A singular fact connected with the physical geography and river system of this part of Java is that the three largest rivers of the island all have their sources within a few miles of the south coast. The sources of the Brantas are absolutely scarcely three miles from it. The island therefore may be described as an inclined plane from south to north, diversified by many large isolated volcanic cones and ash ranges, which may be said to run almost in every direction; but in the centre of the island there are two conspicuous east and west ranges which act as a barrier to the waters flowing down the inclined plane to the north until a gap is found, when they are thrown off towards the east, and disembogue into the large alluvial delta already spoken of.

Between the sources of the Solo, Madiun, and Surabaya Rivers there are two lofty volcanoes whose slopes and dependent ridges cover a very large extent of country: Mount Wilis to the east, 7,086 feet above the level of the sea; and Mount Lawu to the westward, which is very little lower than Semeru, or about 10,100 feet. Both these mountains contribute largely to the sources of the Madiun and Solo; while on the northern slopes of Gunong Wilis two tributaries, one of the Madiun and the other of the Surabaya, are separated only by a narrow ridge of scoriæ.

Solo.—The whole of this mountainous and volcanic region is as wildly picturesque as any country in the world. The immense height of the mountains and their volcanic activity, the marks of nature's convulsions on a truly gigantic scale would alone give a sublime interest to such a territory; but when we add the grandeur as well as the beauty of the vegetation, it truly presents aspects to the traveller which baffle description. The forests of teak and other trees, as useful or as ornamental, the profusion of fruits and flowers, the shrubs and ferns, make it a region which stands alone amongst the wonders of nature. But when we add to this the beauties and varieties of the wild animals, the birds, the insects and the denizens of the seas and rivers, Java becomes almost a fairy-land to the traveller. On the slopes of Mount Lawu at a height of 3,600 feet, and again on another spur at over 4,000 feet are the ruins of the temples of Suku and Chato respectively. These are Hindoo in character, though from their rude and primitive structure, they would seem to have belonged to much less civilized times. However, any speculation is set at rest by an inscription with the date of 1361 of the year of Salivana which is A.D. 1439. The whole of this locality may be said to be the historical land of Java. It is here that the ancient empire of Suracata still exists. The traveller is at once struck in visiting this region with the ancient aspect of things. The costume of the people differs little, and that of the princes and nobles seems to have undergone little alteration since the days in which they were carved in stone on the trachyte walls of Boro-budor.

The valley of the Solo river is bounded on the west by the twin volcanoes of Merapi and Merabu, the first nearly 9,000 and the second nearly 10,000 feet above the level of the sea The city of Jokiakarta lies on the southern slopes of Merapi, or rather on the plain at the foot of the mountains, and a stream which comes from its summit almost, empties itself on the south coast. From the city, which boasts of being the residence of the sultan or king of the province of Jokiakarta, there is a good road of 17 miles length to Galur, an important campong, on the few lowlands of the south coast, formed by the alluvium of the river Songo with its tributaries Krasac, Progo, Tangsie and Ello. This was the only time I was on the southern waters of the island.

JOKIAKARTA.—Jokiakarta is especially interesting to geologists, because of its beds of tertiary marl with fossils. On the river Songo, near Nangulan, about 8 miles west-by-north of the city of Jokiakarta, are beds of marl or limestone associated with Hornblende andesite, claystone, pyrolusite, and brown coal. Possibly these beds may be the equivalents of the tertiary coal deposits and eocene nummulitic limestones of west Sumatra.

Due north of Suracata is the Japara peninsula, on the coast which forms the most northerly portion of the centre of the island. This is entirely due to the large volcano of Murija, about 5,000 feet above sea level, separated from the range already described (which I distinguish as the Ngawi Range) by the valley of the river Tanggul Angin and its tributaries. The main stream empties itself on the west side of the peninsula. The coast slopes away S.S.W. from the mouth of this river to the city of Samarang. The intermediate country is formed of alluvial deposits from the somewhat important rivers Demak, Bujaran, and Agung-bajo. Samarang is the capital of one of the finest provinces of Java, with an area of about 1,425 square miles. It is densely populated, perhaps the most thickly populated of any portion of Java or the Indian Archipelago, including the Philippine Islands. The most of the inhabitants are Javanese, with about 30,000 Chinese and their mixed descendants, and 5,000 Arabs and other nationalities, amongst which there are a majority of natives of Celebes. It is a town which seemed to me next in importance to Surabaya, but far more attractive in appearance, as the streets are wider, more cleanly, and boast of much better buildings. The country around is also much more attractive. There is a pliocene formation with fossils in the province, and also a brown coal of which I saw specimens, though I did not visit the locality.

West of a line drawn north and south from Samarang the island narrows again, but not quite to such restricted limits as in the district of Besuki. The country has physical features which are easily described. It is one mass of small volcanoes mingled with the large peaks of Jeremai (9,500 feet), Slamet (over 10,000 feet), and Jakurag (about 9,200 feet). Of this part of the country I know nothing from personal inspection, except along the coast. There are three large seaports on the north coast, namely, Pekalongan, Tagal and Cheribon, about 50 miles apart; Pekalongan being on the east, Tagal in the centre, and Cheribon on the west. These are the sites of large towns, the capitals of provinces which bear the same names. Though wide in extent they are not by any means amongst the richest provinces of Java. Cheribon may be considered as a province which forms a division between the Javanese and the Sundanese, the western portion of it being peopled by the latter race. The name is said by Crawfurd to be derived from charuban which in Javanese means a mixture. It was at one time an important kingdom in Java next perhaps to Bantam. The country to the south is so exceedingly rugged that it is perfectly unfit for cultivation and is but little known. There is one large river with many tributaries which drains from the slopes of Mount Papandayang in the kingdom of Sunda, and almost on the south coast. The mountain is over 8,000 feet above the level of the sea.

MOUNT PAPANDAYING.—This is the celebrated volcano which, in the year 1772, was the locality of a tremendous earthquake or subsidence in which many people perished. It occurred at midnight between the 11th and 12th of August, beginning with the emission of dense volumes of steam which enshrouded the mountain in thick clouds. Shortly afterwards these clouds became luminous, and the inhabitants, who thickly peopled the lower slopes of the crater, were alarmed by the violent explosion and speedily took to flight ; not however in time to save themselves, as the ground began to open and crack beneath their feet. Shortly afterwards an immense subsidence took place engulphing the most of the mountain and swallowing up the poor inhabitants into the depths of the earth. This was accompanied by a fearful noise, similar to that which happened at the subsidence of Krakatoa, which was heard over 900 miles away. It is estimated that the subsidence extended over an area 15 miles long by 6 wide, and it was said that the old mountain, which was one of the highest if not the highest in the island, had almost entirely disappeared except a few fragments of the lower slopes. From the chasm into which the crater collapsed, immense quantities of ashes, cinders and stones were ejected to a great height red-hot or in a half molten condition. These ejectamenta covered the country around for a great distance, carrying great destruction to life and property. Previous to the disturbance the volcano had been so very quiet that agriculture and settlement had gradually extended up its slopes, and a numerous population was established around. It is supposed that over 40 villages were completely destroyed by the catastrophe. Some of these utterly disappeared by being swallowed up, while the rest were in a great measure covered over by the ashes, cinders and fiery rain. About three thousand people perished, besides cattle, live stock and large and valuable crops of cotton, indigo, Betel-pepper and coffee.* Altogether the eruption was a terribly destructive one, but nothing in comparison with that of Krakatoa in 1883.

CRAWANG.—The northern river, which takes its rise from this volcano, enters into the sea as the Riam Battam on the extreme eastern end of a wide prolongation of the north coast, beginning at Cheribon, and extending westwards to Batavia. The whole of this area is watered by at least ten rivers of various sizes, and gives rise to a large tract of alluvial marshy land of great richness, which forms the province of Crawang, 1538 square miles in extent. The low-lying lands are rich, but rather too marshy to be thickly populated, or at least so thickly as other districts in Java. The largest river, the Ji-Tarum, is the most westerly, and enters into the sea through an extensive delta on the east side of Batavia Bay.

BANTAM.—The rest of the western end of Java comprises the kingdom of Bantam, and its physical description is as follows:— The whole southern side of the island is composed of high volcanic ranges, dependent upon numerous cones which have been ancient points of eruption. The culminating point is Mount Halimun, an active crater about 5,300 feet above the sea. This is connected

---

* "Jaarboek van het Mijnwezen in Nederlandsch Oost-Indië. Pt. I., 1873, p. 114. Also, " Transactions of the Batavian Society of Arts and Sciences." Vol. IX., where there is an account of the eruption by Dr. Horsfield.

by a range to the eastward with Mount Salak (nearly 7,000 feet) and Panjerango (9,300 feet), which is an active crater, forming the eastern termination of the range, which here has a very wide extension southward. These two mountains are familiar to most travellers who visit Java and "*do*" the island by going from Batavia to Buitenzorg. They form one of the most lovely pieces of scenery visible anywhere in this beautiful island. It has been engraved so often as to need no description.

The north side of the kingdom of Bantam is formed of the rich alluvial plains, to the westward of Batavia, deposited by numerous rivers which have their sources in the mountains just referred to. The extreme north-west of the coast of the Straits of Sunda terminates in Mount Karang (5,350 feet) and Mount Pulde Sari (about 3,900 feet).

PHYSICAL GEOGRAPHY.—Briefly, then, the physical geography of Java may be stated thus :—A long and narrow volcanic island extending east and west; high and precipitous for the whole extent of its southern side, and consisting entirely on its northern side of low alluvial and, to some extent, marshy plains. These alluvial plains extend for long distances out to sea where the waters are extremely shallow, and the coast without the protection of any high land. The seas of the southern coast, on the contrary, are very deep, and scarcely affording any shelter for vessels. The high lands of the south coast are entirely formed by volcanic cones, connected with one another only by irregular ash and lava deposits which have flowed from them. Apparently there is no range of elevation apart from the craters, but it suggests itself that the ancient land, if there has been any such, was a range along what is now the southern coast. First of all, it is a watershed without a break of any kind. Secondly, whatever fossiliferous formations are found in the island occur in this range. Thus there are recognised miocene and pliocene rocks, and probably eocene beds as well. There is also a tertiary coal formation, and palæozoic slates and schists or metamorphic strata. There are but few places where these rocks become visible, possibly indicating the narrow limits of the land ere the volcanic outbursts commenced to modify it into its present form. The subsidiary ranges spoken of in the centre of the island appear to be entirely of volcanic origin. They are of small extent, and are pierced in one case by a large river. It is, however, to be borne in mind that in general direction they correspond with the main divide, which is the axial direction of the island, and of the volcanic fissure extending through so many islands to the eastward before it finally turns to the north towards the Philippine Islands.

One remarkable feature connected with the volcanic disturbance manifested in Java has been the part played by subsidence in the formation of craters. All of the mountains on the eastern side of the island have upon their summits craters of very large dimensions. In the preceding pages many instances of this have been given, so that it will be only necessary to mention Tengger, which is by no means the largest. Dr. Horsfield has left us a sensational description of this, which shows what it was in his time.

BROMO.—"This mountain," he says, "constitutes one of the most remarkable volcanoes of the island. It rises from a very large base by a gentle slope with gradually ascending ridges. The summit, seen from a distance, is less conical than most of the other principal volcanoes, varying in height at different points from 7,000 to 8,000 feet. The crater is not at the summit but more than 1000 feet below the highest point, and consists of a large excavation of an irregularly circular form, surrounded on all sides by a range of hills of different elevations. It is by far the largest crater in the island, and probably exceeds in size every other crater existing on the globe. It constitutes an immense gulf, the bottom of which is level and denominated by the natives the dasar (the floor). This is naked of vegetation, and covered with sand throughout. In one portion in the middle, the sand is loose, and blown by the wind into slight ridges. To this the natives give the name of Sagarawadi, literally "sea of sand."

The largest diameter of the entire crater is, according to my estimate, full three miles. From the interior, near the middle, rise several conical peaks or distinct volcanoes. The chief of these, the mountain Brama (in Sanskrit, the god Brama, or fire), is a perfectly regular cone and still in partial activity, with occasional eruptions. It is surrounded, on one side, by the sea of sand above mentioned. Adjoining it stands another conical peak, more than 1,000 feet high, named Watangan (the Javanese Campus martius), or Widadaren (abode of celestial nymphs), covered externally with sand, quite naked, and, on account of its steepness the top has never been examined. At a small distance from the Brama rises a smaller cone, called Butak ("the bald"). The two last have not exhibited any activity in recent times. * * * The soil of the Tenger hills is extremely fertile consisting of a deep vegetable mould, accumulated for many ages on the sand and débris thrown up from the mountain. Vegetables of northern latitudes, potatoes, cabbages, onions, &c., are planted by the natives in great abundance, for the supply of the markets of Pasuruhan and Surabaya. European fruits, as apples and peaches are also raised, as well as wheat and other northern grains. Rice refuses to grow, and the cocoa-nut produces no fruit" (Geographical Preface and Postscript of "Plantæ Javanicæ rariores," 1852).

This was the description of the crater as Dr. Horsfield saw it in 1825. The following are my own experiences in September, 1883, when with two European companions I visited the sand sea from Tosari. We started early in the morning with a guide and two coolies carrying necessary supplies, of which water was one, for there was none to be had in the crater. The road was an open carriage-way for four miles, and then became a wide bridle-track, which descended into a thickly-wooded gorge. Here we saw many wild pea-fowls, and the forest resounded with their cries. There were no campongs, but plenty of those elegant bamboo houses by the side of the stream which flowed through the valley. The picturesque steep roofs, with the ornamental vertical gable reminded one of Swiss chalets. The temperature, too, reminded one of them, for it was very cold, though clear. We soon again ascended into a treeless region. The grass was thick and rank, for there was no cultivation. It could easily be seen that we were approaching the scene of more active disturbance. The short billow-like hillock of ash grew more irregular and steep. Here, also, I saw many species of plants and ferns which I obtained nowhere else. A rather steeper climb than usual brought us to a miserable attap shed, built on a terrace cut out of the rock, and fenced in. All beyond and below that was then a white sea of mist, out of which came a dull, hoarse roar from Bromo.

We were on the edge of the large crater. Below us was the mysterious sand sea, and in the middle of that Bromo. It was scarcely eight in the morning, and the clouds had not cleared away. Above our heads the sky was shining brightly, but below all was like white wool. To the southward was Semeru, also shrouded in mist. While waiting for the morning to clear I took the bearings and altitudes of those peaks which showed, with the aid of a prismatic compass and pocket sextant. By the observations made going and returning I found the rest-house to be 7,237 feet above the sea.

I was just finishing with my water-boiling when the mist began to roll back. In ten minutes all had cleared away, and a scene emerged so rigid and severe that it was hard to understand how it had been concealed under those soft white fleecy clouds. But what a wonderful—what a desolate scene it was! An immense wide plain appeared 500 feet below us—so immediately below us that one would imagine it was easy to leap into it from the terrace where we halted. It was, in truth, a sand sea of greyish-brown, with rugged walls of slag and cinder all round. Sometimes these walls were blackened or reddened by fire, but more often grey and scored by the rains as if they consisted of fresh mortar. The sand sea seemed level and devoid of vegetation, though there is grass upon it. The creeks of last year's rains had made wide channels of ripple marks across the plain. They looked as if filled with running water, but they were perfectly dry, and so

was everything in this arid basin. From the further end a
winding track or road can be seen descending the hill-sides and
crossing the floor of the crater. This is the Probolingo road
which joins our road at the rest-house. I need not say that
there are no trees or even a blackened, stunted bush. Scattered
tufts of sedges grow here and there, but not sufficient to
redeem the general aspect of sterility. The whole reminds one of
unfinished excavations on a stupendous scale. In the middle of
the floor is a steep conical hill, some 1,000 feet high, clothed with
timber and yet scored by rains so as to leave deep ruts, crevices,
and gullies of white or grey ash. Half hidden by this hill is
Bromo. It is a lower cone, truncated, and wide. It is absolutely
destitute of vegetation, and of a uniform whitish grey, darker
than snow, and yet somehow bringing it to mind. The crater is
backed by a higher and more rugged mountain with a still colder
wintry aspect. The view is cheerless, indeed, as there is not a sign
of life, either animal or vegetable. From the centre of Bromo
rises a thick white smoke. It rises rapidly as if impelled by heat,
and is thin or dense according as the bubbling noise of the crater
is faint or uproarious. It is nearly 3 miles from where we stood,
and we could feel the vibration very distinctly under our feet.
Fortunately there were neither ashes nor stones ejected on that
day, so we could make the ascent safely.

Five hundred feet of a descent on a bridle path, which
made short zigzags in loose ash, brought us to the floor of
the sand sea. Nothing but a Javanese pony would keep
his foot upon it. Not that one could ride down. Blondin
might, but all mankind are not so gifted in preserving a
balance. It is no use troubling my readers with the process
of staggering knee-deep in ash, which rises round one
almost to suffocation. There are places where a false step might
be fatal, but we did not manage to fall over these, yet falls we had
plenty, and so must anyone, for there is no way of getting down
except by sliding and falling.

But just before we left the platform the mist had rolled away
from Semeru. It now appeared a grand mountain rising close to

us to a height which looked great even to us, elevated as we were. It seemed about 14 miles away. While we were gazing at its outlines a sudden eruption burst from its summit. First came a volume of black smoke, which rolled over and over like a turban as it rose up into the sky. As this spread a fierce fountain of ash and stones shot up underneath it and soon beyond it, making a grey and black canopy to the cone. So furious was the outburst that in a few seconds it was more than 3,000 feet above the summit. With our glasses we could easily discern the grey or white ash slipping in refts and avalanches down the side of the mountain peak caused either by the fall of stones or by the unceasing rain of pumice. This became thicker and thicker as the eruption went on, and soon a thick curtain of ash and smoke hung between us and the magnificent outline of Semeru. We listened for some distant thunderings from this fiery outbreak, but all was merged in the hoarse roaring and bubbling of Bromo in the valley below. I never shall forget the sublimity of the scene of the first explosion. The clear outline of the mountain, so bright in the early morning, its grand height and graceful proportions, and then the sudden disturbance of its calm repose by outbreak of ash, smoke, and fire until all was submerged in cloud, made it surely one of the grandest of natural phenomena.

The sight of this eruption rendered us more anxious to have a better view of the active crater near. We descended into the sand sea as already related. When we arrived on the level our state from dust and ash was rather ludicrous. The land beneath our feet was nearly of the uniform black hue which our faces, hands, and clothes had very soon assumed. But it was now a level plain that we were upon, and our course towards Bromo was easy and rapid. We were in a perfect amphitheatre of large dimensions. The walls around us were generally 500 and sometimes 1,000 feet high, apparently quite rugged and precipitous, except in one or two places. Their rough irregular outline, their varieties of colour, such as an old furnace wall or kiln might present, made them picturesque but wild and savage in aspect. It is in fact just like the walls of an immense smoked and blackened cauldron. No one can have any difficulty in seeing that it cannot be so long ago since the sand sea was a seething mass of lava. This extinct outer crater or sand sea is almost 5 miles long by a mile and a-half or perhaps more at its widest part. It is probably a crater of subsidence, as the broken strata of the cliffs all round would seem to testify. To any one who would give the necessary expenditure of time, measurements would easily show what has been the former height and form of the cone.

We skirted round the hill or cone which occupies the centre of the sand sea, evidently a crater built up by a hasty and violent eruption. It is somewhat thickly clothed with wild oak, chestnut, and other trees, but in places the loose grey ash has been rather deeply scored by the rains. I should say that the hill was almost inaccessible, though Mr. Weld-Blundell offered to scale it within six hours if we would wait for him. Our guides assured us that no one had been on the top. It can, however, be scarcely over 1,000 feet above the level of the sand sea.

Having passed two-thirds round this cone we came to a well-built temporary attap tent, with a shed of the same material close by. Both of these were covered with half-withered adornments of flowers, coloured paper, red calico, &c. There were marks too of a rather extensive encampment. These were the remains of the annual festival held by the mountaineers in honour of the god Brama, after whom the mountain is named. Flowers, fruit, and wine are offered on the mountain, and then thrown into the crater as a peace offering. Music with various other festivities keep up the celebration for two or three days. They say that 10,000 people and more assemble in the sand sea on these occasions, including, strangely enough, many Mahometan Javanese, whose creed utterly condemns such rites.

Rising in a slope a short distance from this old camp were slopes and hillocks of grey ash, having much the appearance of hills of blown sand by the side of the ocean. Scattered over them irregularly were nodules of pumice and scoriæ, seldom larger than 2 inches in diameter. Some of these had been quite recently ejected, showing that it is not always safe to be in the neighbourhood of the crater. After about half a-mile or so of gradually ascending hillocks of grey ash, the crater wall suddenly rises into a steep truncated cone, between 200 and 300 feet above the slope. It would be almost impossible to ascend so steep an incline of loose ash as fine as the finest dust; but the Javanese have constructed for their own purpose a very simple and ingenious staircase or ladder of bamboo. By this means the side of the cone can be scaled without more difficulty than the fatigue of a long steep climb, viz. a ladder, where one-third of the rounds are wanting, making only steps or jumps, at times rather long. It is strange that this ladder, or a similar one, has been there from time immemorial. Dr. Horsfield saw it nearly 70 years ago. It is used by the priests at the annual sacrifice, at which period it is renewed or repaired. It needed considerable repair at the present time.

It would be difficult to convey an idea of the wintry, desolate aspect which this part of the crater presents. There is not a trace of vegetation. If here and there a weed or a blade of grass shows itself it is speedily covered by the fine, almost imperceptible, rain of dust and ash from the crater, which goes on for ever. The roar heard at the foot of the ladder makes one unaccustomed to it pause. There is nothing like it, unless the din and hoarse echoes of a huge steam factory; but then the sharp crackling kind of bubble which shakes the ground and dominates all is peculiarly its own. The blue sulphurous fumes which are rising from the crater seem light and etherial, as seen from below. From the rest-house they appeared dense and suffocating.

There were no stones or ashes falling on our side. Even the smoke and steam was blown by the wind to nearly the opposite margin; but there was very little wind. The fumes rose up to a great height, and spread like a canopy before they were stirred at all. Up we went, having fastened our ponies to bamboo stakes

would end before we were half way to the top. At length we
stood upon the perilous brink, where a very necessary handrail
a few yards long has been left by the considerate mountaineers.
The sight at first is enough to make one dizzy. One looks down a
funnel-shaped chasm about 500 feet deep, with an awfully steep
incline. The sides are encrusted with yellow sulphur, and various
huge stains of red, white and black. One sees also that much of
what seems like smoke is in reality steam, for there are constant
runnels of water flowing down the ash bank into the basin, and
scoring the sides in every conceivable way. At the summit it is
about one-third of a mile across; at the bottom about a third of
that, or less. One part of the bottom is merely mud, from which
steam bubbles rise. On the side beneath us there is a deep wide
chasm, in which the smoke, ash, and steam conceal all but the
blackened and sulphur-encrusted rim. From this comes the hoarse,
deafening roar, which is really quite appalling. As the steam
rises, much of the ash falls back from the cloud, giving the sides a
weeping or combed-out appearance like a fountain of spray. All
round the outlet the mud has formed a rim, which has spread from
time to time, and then been cut down by the streams of condensed
water. We tried to throw stones down into the pit. There were
plenty of large fragments of scoriæ to hand, but the ash was so
fine and loose that, after rolling a short distance amid clouds of
dust, the stones buried themselves and became immovable. Once
or twice we fancied that we managed to sling a small stone into
the opening and that the roar became louder; but we could not be
sure of this, for nothing could be seen. The ash looks solid enough,
but one sinks ankle deep into it, and every now and then it slides
away from under the feet.

The opposite side to where we stood is much higher and forms
a kind of peak, and then stretches away to form the sides of a
larger but extinct crater to the south, Widaderen, or the abode
of celestial nymphs. Like the other extinct cone (Butak, or the
bald, though it is not bald now), neither of these cones has been
in activity within historic times. I tried to walk round the rim
of the crater to Widaderen, but had to give up the attempt. The

walk is so narrow that a very light puff of wind might take one over in either direction. Besides this, considerable masses of ash were continually slipping away, either down the steep exterior wall or into the crater. If an unfortunate pedestrian happened to slip with these avalanches of cinders he would scarcely reach the bottom without being suffocated. He might as well fall into a bin full of fine flour. If, however, he did reach the bottom alive, not "all the king's horses nor all the king's men" would pull him up again.

It does not appear that there is any great risk in ascending Bromo, yet the scattered stones around attest that at intervals the projectiles are flying up and down in a manner rather embarrassing to the peaceful sightseer. Once or twice we got just a little whiff of the sulphurous fumes of insufferable odour which on me at least produced the effect of violent coughing. They say that some visitors have paid the forfeit of their lives by approaching too near in times of unusual activity, but I could get no particulars. On the other hand, more than one European resident has assured me that the mountaineers have been known to descend to the bottom of the crater by means of rattan ropes. I am very incredulous about this. In the first place, I don't see how they could manage to make their way down the slope of fine ash, which, as I have said, is like flour, and in which even small stones were soon buried. In the next place, I don't see how any human being would find breathing air at the bottom of such a pit.

One can but speculate as to what makes the roaring noise at the bottom of the chasm. It sounds like the bubbling of some fierce incandescent mass. Yet I do not think that the molten matter can be very near. No doubt this volcano is connected with the great underground sea or lake of lava which has so many boisterous outlets for its stream and fires throughout the island. But the depth at which this liquid reservoir lies must be great, probable much below the sea level. This would make it perhaps two miles or more below the rise of the crater of Bromo. The orifice is, therefore, a kind of steam-pipe for the escape of pent-up vapour. There has never been any large outflow of lava from this crater or any of its older portions. Ash, steam, and cinders have been the only ejectamenta during the greater part of its history. Melted lava might sometimes be forced up this sole narrow opening, but the force required to raise such a liquid volume would be great, and it is hard to suppose that it would stop there. As a matter of fact ash eruptions have been the rule, and lava the exception in the island of late years.

Measurements have shown that the floor of the crater is higher by over 100 feet than it was in 1845. This is easily accounted for by the accumulation of ash. Sometimes a perfect cone forms round the opening, but this is sure to be blown away in periods of more violent activity. It is at such times that the crater is dangerous to approach. With the exception of such occasional paroxysms it does not appear that there has been of late years any extra violence manifested by the volcano.

I must say that there is something dissappointing in the aspect of this volcano. One expects to see a little of the ocean of fire at the bottom of the pit from which steam and ashes are emitted with such a roaring noise; but instead a chasm is all that is dimly visible through the refts in the vapour. But it is always so when such perilous phenomena can be inspected at all. Were the sea of fire boiling with its fierce glow at the bottom of the crater, one dare not even approach its foot, much less stand upon its brink. So we must be content with craters as we find them.

It was an easy journey down to the embankment, where we had good reason to be thankful for the homely shelter which the votaries of Brama afforded us. Here we camped in peace and security, watching the glorious tints of sunset over this strange and wild scene. There is nothing to remain all night for. The crater is not lit up with any glow. The mist, which after nightfall spreads like a curtain over the valley, does not even grant one the luxury of a star-lit sky. But the roar of the crater through the darkness of the night fills one with as much awe as the heavens with their silent eloquence.

VOLCANIC ERUPTIONS.—The history of terrible eruptions and volcanic catastrophes in Java would make a book in itself, while the destruction of life and property on a large scale in different parts of the island have been awfully frequent. In October, 1822, a crater close to Papandayang burst out with such suddenness into eruption that deep night seemed to come without warning upon the midst of a hot summer's day. The darkness was accompanied with a deluge of hot water and mud which spouted out, sweeping all before it, and causing fearful devastation amid animal and vegetable life for miles around. The ashes and stones covered the ground even 40 miles away. But strange to say the eruption only lasted a few hours and then all was still for four days. Just as the people were recovering from their terror the mountain burst forth into activity again, beginning with a violent earthquake which broke down the mountain, leaving in its place an enormous incomplete crater. The deluges of mud and stone reappeared, but this time with great blocks of basalt which were carried many miles away. The whole face of nature was changed in consequence, for there was no record of any previous activity in this crater, and a dense jungle forest covered the whole area. Over 100 villages were destroyed, and about 4,000 persons are supposed to have perished.

Equally terrible earthquakes are recorded; as, for instance, one in Batavia in 1699, and another quite recently in Jokiakarta and the neighbourhood, sacrificing thousands of lives. This was in 1867. But probably the most awful catastrophe of which there is any record in Java is that of Krakatoa, in the Straits of Sunda, which took place on August 27th, 1883. I was in Java at this time, though not in the immediate neighbourhood of the volcano; yet I saw many of the terrible evidences of its disastrous effects.

The crater of Krakatoa, which is on an island about 25 miles from the west end of Java, and 14 from the south of Sumatra, has been in a kind of smouldering activity as long as the island has been known to Europeans. In May, 1883, it broke out into activity, sending forth showers of ashes, stones, and mud, accompanied with violent explosions. These phenomena gradually increased in severity till the beginning of August, when the country for 100 miles and more began to be covered with the ashes. On Sunday, the 27th, Batavia was rendered quite dark, while the explosions were so loud as to be heard in some directions nearly 1,000 miles distant. An immense amount of material was thrown up, and this, no doubt, was causing a stupendous cavity in the crater. At 2 a.m. on Monday the crater collapsed, and subsided with a roaring noise of such terrific intensity as to defy all attempt at description. The regurgitation of the sea into the crater caused two tidal waves 80 or 90 feet high to break upon the coast of Java, utterly devastating the country, destroying many towns and villages, and sweeping over 50,000 people into eternity. Such a catastrophe has no parallel in modern history. The whole coast of western Java was changed beyond recognition: roads, light-houses, and buildings of all kinds disappeared, while at Krakatoa the sea over one part of the crater is more than 100 fathoms in depth. The portions of the ancient cone which remain form broken, detached, rocky islands, quite different from their former position and shape, so that a new survey of the locality became immediately necessary.

The former condition of Krakatoa was that it consisted of one large island, whose greatest diameter was nearly north and south, with a high volcanic cone on the south end. At each side of its northern termination, almost touching it, were two smaller islands, Verlatan and Lang. At present Krakatoa has disappeared, except the peak at the south end of the island, which has been bisected by the subsidence, leaving a precipice over 1000 feet high, formed of ash and scoriæ, with the usual volcanic ejectamenta which form the highest side of craters; what little is left of the island now has its greatest diameter from east to west, with soundings of from 102 to 106 fathoms on its northeast side. Verlatan and Lang Islands still exist in the same positions and about the same dimensions, but Verlatan is surrounded with a number of rocks, reefs, and shoals on the side of the former site of Krakatoa. The soundings hereabouts are otherwise the same; but there is a general subsidence of the sea-bottom around the island in the directions of Sumatra and Java, giving depths of 60 and 80 fathoms, where formerly 40 to 50 fathoms was the extreme. A mile south of Krakatoa 126 fathoms were obtained, where 80 was the former record.

HOT SPRINGS.—As might naturally be expected, the hot springs and wells of Java present most interesting phenomena. At Surabaya, in the midst of the alluvial flats, there is a petroleum well which, I think, like many others of its kind, is connected with immense deposits of drift-wood in the mud beneath. The hot springs and mud springs are numerous, but especially worthy of mention are those of Grobogan, situated about 30 miles east in a straight line from Samarang. They are seldom visited by travellers, but deserve careful investigation. The most convenient way to reach them is to go by railway from Samarang to the Gundik station, from whence there is a fair road due north $15\frac{1}{2}$ miles to Purwodadi, one of the important towns of the province of Japara. Five miles more of a carriage road brings one to Grobogan, a village or campong to the south of a small east and west limestone range. In the valleys between the spurs from this range on the south side there are many hot springs emitting both mud and steam. About the centre of the range is a mud geyser which in Horsfield's time emitted periodical explosions of mud and steam, but is much more intermittent in character now. Horsfield's description is as follows:—

"About the centre of this limestone district is found an extraordinary volcanic phenomenon. On approaching it from a distance it is first discovered by large volumes of smoke rising and disappearing at intervals of a few seconds, resembling the vapours arising from a violent surf; while a dull noise is heard like that of distant thunder. Having advanced so near that the vision is no longer impeded by the smoke, a large hemispherical mass is observed, consisting of black earth mixed with water, about 16 feet in diameter, rising to the height of 20 or 30 feet, in a perfectly regular manner and as it were pushed up by force beneath, which suddenly explodes with a dull noise, and scatters about a volume of black mud in every direction. After an interval of a few seconds the hemispherical body of mud or earth rises and explodes again. This volcanic ebullition goes on uninterruptedly, throwing up a globular body of mud and dispersing it with violence through the neighbouring plain. The spot where the ebullition occurs is nearly circular and perfectly level. It is covered only with the earthy particles impregnated with salt water which are thrown up from below. Its circumference may be estimated at about half an English mile. In order to conduct the salt water to the circumference, small passages or gutters are made in the loose muddy earth, which convey it to the borders, where it is collected in holes dug in the ground for the purpose of evaporation. A strong, pungent, sulphurous smell, somewhat resembling that of earth-oil, is perceived on standing near the explosion, and the mud recently thrown up, possesses a degree of heat exceeding that of the surrounding atmosphere. During the rainy season these explosions are more violent, the mud is thrown up much higher, and the noise heard at a greater distance. This volcanic phenomenon is situated near the centre of the large plain, and the large series of volcanoes, and owes its origin to the general cause of the numerous volcanic eruptions which occur in the island." (Transactions of the Batavian Society of Arts and Sciences, Vol. IX.). This singular phenomenon is known to the Javanese under the name of Kuwu, as is also the village of salt-makers near it. In Jaranese the word simply means "place of abode." But in Javanese legend the eruption is supposed to be produced by a fabulous monster snake, of which the place is supposed to be the dwelling. Grobogan was also the seat of the ancient Javanese kingdom." (Crawfurd's Descriptive Dictionary of the Indian Islands, p. 146).

In concluding this brief notice of the physical structure of Java it may be stated that, beyond all comparison, it is the most interesting and attractive island of the Indian Archipelago. The immense height and rugged character of its mountains give its scenery a sublime beauty. The almost exclusively volcanic soils make a vegetation of incomparable luxuriance. On this account a wild stony character is imparted to by far the greater portion of the island, but the remainder or the alluvial plains have a richness with which no country in the world can vie. Thus it is able to support an enormous population for so small an island, there being 19 or 20 millions on the soil, and extreme poverty is a thing unknown.

CLIMATE.—The climate of Java is easily described; being in the monsoon region of the tropics the seasons succeed one another with perfect regularity, alternating between the north-west and south-west monsoons. The first of these is the rainy season which averages about 90 inches per annum, though in particular situations, especially where the climate is modified by the mountains, it is greater or less as in other lands. The temperature seldom rises to 90° and during the day on the plains is about 85° in the shade. Speaking from my own experience, I found the heat of Java more bearable than any portion of India or the Indian Archipelago. I believe it is unhealthy, solely on account of the bad systems or no-systems of drainage. The open and foul ditches interlacing the most crowded thoroughfares of Surabaya and Samarang not only account for the insalubrity of the places, but make one marvel that they are not much worse. But Europeans are scarcely able to cope with the apathy of orientals on the subject of sanitary precautions.

The convenience of having almost a temperate climate within easy reach is found on the slopes or plateaux of the numerous mountain elevations. In this way Java is enabled to have a supply of European vegetables, a luxury unknown almost in any of the other portions of the Indian Archipelago. About 5,000 feet above the level of the sea the slopes of countless valleys on the Tengger and Semeru are covered with extensive kitchen-gardens in which cabbages of every variety, lettuces, potatoes, peas, beans, cucumbers, turnips, &c., are found in great luxuriance. The Tengger is also used as a sanatorium for European colonists; the Javanese, like most orientals, do not take kindly to climbing mountains. As a rule the climates at this elevation are chilly, foggy and damp. I found the mountain regions always depressing, especially as in these latitudes the sun is seldom seen at such elevations. It is rarely also, one gets a glimpse at the plains below.

VEGETATION.—Only a few words can be here devoted to the vegetation of Java, as to attempt to enter into any detail would be quite disproportionate to this essay. In brief it may be said that Java is, in the main characters of its flora, like the whole of the Indian Archipelago. On the coast are found the dense mangrove forests (*Bruguiera, Rhizophora &c.*). In the plains cultivation leaves but little to the indigenous flora. Useful palms are introduced, fruit trees, such as mangoes, mangosteens, durians, bread-fruit, jack-fruit, custard-apples, rambi, rambutan, guavas, jambosa, pine-apples, and last not least, every variety of plantain and banana. I do not refer to the cultivation which includes coffee, tea, quinine, indigo, sugar, Betel-pepper, pepper, spices generally, cotton, sweet potatoes, tobacco, and earth-nuts, and rice in enormous quantities yet not sufficient for the home consumption.

On the higher slopes of the mountain the jungle commences, with fig-trees, dipterocarpaceous forests interspersed with oaks, chestnuts, the copal tree, a huge king of the forest attaining 150 feet high, and 10 or 12 feet at the bole. This is called by the Malays Dammar and hence the botanical name *Dammara orientalis*, Lambert. The timber is of little value, but it produces a fine transparent resin which deeply coats the ground for yards around and hangs like icicles about the stem, being a source of profit to the natives. The forests in these higher regions are thickly matted together by creepers, vines, climbing palms and aroids of every sort and size, the natural order Melastomaceæ having the largest number of representatives (*Melastoma, Medinilla Sonerila, &c.*). Underneath the trees the shade is thick, making a greenish twilight in which immense tree-ferns and large ferns of the genera *Marattia*, *Angiopteris* and *Matonia*, combined with innumerable other cryptogams cover the ground, while orchids in multitudes of individuals and species cling to the branches and stems of the trees.

The smaller flowers carpet the earth still closer to the ground, including *Didymocarpus, Begonia, Selaginella, Caladium, Maranta*, with luxuriant mosses and lichens.

Between six and seven thousand feet the forests cease, and grasses, ferns and stunted trees are irregularly scattered over the ash deposits. I remember being much struck at seeing groves of *Casuarina littoralis* on the road sides of Tengger at about 6,000 feet of elevation; but I think these trees must have been introduced; they are indigenous on the coast in many parts of the Indian Archipelago. On this treeless region some alpine plants are found such as *Rhododendron, Vaccinium*, and a pink primrose (*Primula imperialis*), which was once exclusively confined to Mount Papandayong, but is now found elsewhere as a result of cultivation. The *Nepenthes* or pitcher plants are found in similar localities.

The Javanese flora has an advantage over that of most of the Archipelago, in being nearly completely known. Horsfield, Blume, Miquel, Grevelink, Filet, Teysmann, Binnendijk, Kurz, Wallich, Jack and others have celebrated and described its beauties and richness in costly publications, some richly illustrated.

ZOOLOGY.—The natural history of Java is rich and peculiar. The majority of its mammalia, which Wallace supposes to number about 90 distinct kinds, are identical with those of Sumatra and Borneo; but Java has no tapir, elephant, Malay bear, or orangutan. The Javanese rhinoceros and hare are identical with species found in Indo-China. Of 240 species of land-birds 40 are not known out of Java, while some of the common and characteristic Indian birds, such as Indian magpies (*Dendrocitta*), the green gaper (*Calyptomena*), the bearded roller (*Nyctiornis*), the argus pheasant, the fire-backed pheasant, and the crested partridge are not known in the island. "On the other hand, there are twelve Javan birds whose nearest allies (sometimes the identical species) occur in the Indo-Chinese countries or the Himalayas, while they are quite unknown in Sumatra and Borneo,

the most popular example of which is the pea-fowl of Java, found also in Siam and Burmah, but not in the intervening islands."*
"Two species of jungle-fowl inhabit the island, one not known further eastward than Sumbawa, the other supposed to be the original stock of all domestic poultry. There is a peacock and several species of partridge and quail, and some very beautiful pigeons, pre-eminent among which is the mountain fruit-dove (*Ptilopus roseicollis*), whose entire head and neck are of an intense rosy pink, contrasting exquisitely with its otherwise green plumage."

The wild animals are very numerous, especially on the lower slopes of the eastern end of Java. Tigers are dangerously abundant there, as well as leopards and black panthers, the latter being only a black variety of the leopard. The rhinoceros is common on the marshy lands at both sides of the island, there being two species; but, strange to say, one of them (*Rhinoceros javanicus*) is not found in other typical Malayan regions, though it reappears in the Indo-Chinese countries. The elephant is not wild, nor is it used as a beast of burden. As might be expected in a country where beasts of prey are so numerous, game is abundant too. There are many species of deer in the woods, besides a wild ox and two species of wild swine. Monkeys of several kinds are well represented, principally Gibbons, Macaques, and *Semnopithecus*. In the western and central parts of the island crowds of the latter are seen passing from tree to tree with great rapidity, chattering as they subsist on the wild fruits. The orang-utan, as already stated, is unknown. There is a wild dog, as in the Malay Peninsula, probably the same species; and a fruit-eating bat of large size, whose habits are scarcely nocturnal, nor is it so gregarious as the species of flying-fox so well known in Australia.

---

*I take these facts generally from the Dutch naturalists as given by Wallace in his "Geographical Distribution of Animals," Vol. I., p. 349. Being no sportsman, my knowledge of the avi-fauna of Java is entirely derived from books and museums, but I regret to add there were no public collections in Java up to 1875.

Ethnology.—There are in Java many different kingdoms, but principally three well-defined and distinct races—namely, the Sundanese on the west, the Jawa or Javanese in the centre, and the Madurese on the east, in the island of that name. In the eastern end of Java also, about Banjuwangi, there is a considerable admixture of Balinese from the neighbouring island of Bali. These races have fairly marked characters, though it requires a long residence and experience for a European to distinguish them. The following are the impressions made upon me:—The Sundanese are slight and graceful, with lighter complexions and particularly mild expression of countenance. The Javanese are short of stature, with the Malay projecting lips and flattened upturned noses strongly marked. The Madurese are a very swarthy, muscular race, evidently well fitted for labour and strength, for which they bear a reputation.

Formerly Java was divided into important kingdoms, some portions of the history of which combine with those of the world of latter times. Originally founded with an advanced civilization from the Indian peninsula, they were converted in the 15th century from Buddhism or Brahminism to Islamism by Arab missionaries. Ever since the Arabs have been somewhat largely domiciled in the island, and an Arab element is engrafted on the language. Annual pilgrimages to Mecca serve to keep up these relations.

At present all the native princes, the king of Jokiakarta and emperor of Solo are under the dominion of the Dutch, who administer their kingdoms for them and give them a liberal maintenance. The splendours of these oriental courts are perhaps as great as ever they were, with all the gaudy adornment, bright coloured silks, birds' feathers, golden umbrellas, and a moderate proportion of gold, silver and precious stones. The pageantry of these relics of the past is mostly interesting to the student and the antiquarian. The rajahs may be distinguished by a pleasing and amiable exterior of marked Indian characters, while their mild-eyed crowds of attendants have the spiritless yet kind look of all the Javanese. Everywhere one meets with courtesy and more marks of respect than in any other part of Malaysia.

The Arabs and Chinese are made to reside in certain parts of every town where they are sufficiently numerous. They are under a captain of their own countrymen who is responsible to the government for their good behaviour. They are confined to certain provinces, outside of which they are not allowed to travel without a special permit. An ex-Resident told me that he had never once given this permission during all the time of his administration. The Chinese and Arabs are under many restrictions, but the former may be said to have all the business of the country in their hands. No native prince or rajah can vie with the splendours of the establishments of certain Chinese merchants of Batavia, Surabaya and Samarang.

Altogether the dense population of Java and its various nationalities are as contented and prosperous as any in the world. The Dutch have done wonders for the island. Splendid roads and various other advantages of cultivation make it a garden of utility and beauty, far in advance of every island in the Archipelago. Having seen the most of them, I know none that can be in any way compared with it.

LANGUAGES.—There are principally three languages in Java besides, on the coast, a certain amount of Malay, which, as Mr. Crawfurd said years ago, is truly the Italian of the East. The native languages are those of Sunda, Java proper and Madura. The Sundanese is spoken by the inhabitants of the mountainous districts of Java west and south-west of Tegal; the Jawa or Javan belongs to the centre of the island and is met with east of Cheribon; the Madurese belongs to that island, and the people who have emigrated therefrom. These languages with that of Bali, Lampong (Sumatra) and Malay, are all dialects of one tongue of which the roots are said to be invariably Sanskrit. The Javanese possess further a classic language or language of literature distinct from the ordinary language of the country. There is a somewhat extensive literature connected with it. It has an alphabet from which the alphabet in use is derived. It is written from left to right and is the same in Madura and Bali. In Java they write with Indian ink, but in Bali the natives use an iron style and cut letters on a Borassus palm leaf, cabbage palm or Pandanus in the same manner as in western India. The leaves are about two inches wide and 18 inches long, and are strung together like a Venetian blind. The letters are formed with the utmost neatness, and together with the illustrations form interesting and valuable records.

It is supposed by Crawfurd that the Sundanese dialect is the most ancient, and probably contains many of the elements of the aboriginal language found amongst the tribes which were conquered by the Hindoos when they established themselves in the island. It may be mentioned also that the Arab elements in the language are confined to less than 100 words, and these mostly terms connected with articles of trade and commerce. The Malay, used as a means of communication between the different nationalities on the coast, differs slightly from the Malay of the Peninsula.

RELIGION AND ANTIQUITIES.-The Javanese profess the Mahometan religion, but mixed up with a good deal of old traditions and superstitions of their former belief. Thus they readily make offerings of flowers and fruits to the idols of Siva, Vishnu, Brahma, and Ganesha, which are still to be found abundantly scattered amongst the ruins of temples in various parts of the island. They do not adhere to the Islam rule of abstaining from stimulants, though they are a temperate race. In this respect the Malay races are remarkably superior to the Hindoos.

The ruins which are found in Java are monuments of great beauty and excellence. The best are at Brambanan, Singosari and Borobodor, besides the whole of the valley of the countries around Borobodor already referred to. A wonderfully detailed history of ancient Java, its manners and customs, could be gathered from the skilful carvings on the entablatures of the ruins. They are mostly from 400 to 500 years old. There are also still more ancient ruins found in various parts of Java; in fact the whole country is rich in oriental antiquities. As usual in such cases it is disputed whether the worship represented in these remains is that of Brahma, Buddha, or Jain. The best investigations on the subject are shut from the knowledge of mankind by being enshrined in the mysteries of the Dutch language.

This completes my notes on the geography of Java, made during lengthened visits, traversing the island from east to west; and, secondly, returning overland from Batavia to Samarang, and thence to Brambanan for a detailed examination of the ruins which I had hurriedly passed by on a former occasion. I also made two journeys through the Sundanese country, taking in all the important towns and objects of interest. I had letters of recommendation to the Governor, but except calling on His Excellency and on one or two of the Residents, all my journeys and investigations were conducted at my own expense. The best season for visiting Java is just before the break-up of the southwest monsoon in August and September.

BANKA AND BINTANG.

After my first visit to Java in 1883, my intention was to explore some portions of the Malay Peninsula. Leaving Batavia I proceeded across the Straits of Sunda to the Straits of Banka, spending a short time at Muntok, the principal town on the island of Banka. This island lies just north of the equator at the south-eastern end of the island of Sumatra, from which it is only separated by a narrow strait. The extent is 120 by 60, with an area of 3568 geographical miles. A low mountain chain, whose highest point is Mount Maras (2000 feet above the sea) runs through the whole island. The rock-formation is granite, giving rise to a barren soil; but yet the country is covered with a dense forest and jungle, mingled with swamps and small streams only navigable for native craft. The island is very rich in alluvial deposits of tin, iron, and native gold. On the edge of the coast I noticed here and there lying upon the granite outliers a palæozoic formation with schists, slates, flagstones, quartzites, and a little limestone, all much metamorphosed and very rich in iron. The decomposition of this rock gives rise to highly ferruginous beds, which English people are accustomed to distinguish generally by the name of laterite. It is at the junction of these beds with the granite that the rich deposits of alluvial tin occur. Banka and the neighbouring island Biliton have long been famous for their rich mines of stream tin; but there are no veins. This forms the great export of these islands, from which the Dutch derive very large revenues. The tin mines of Biliton and Banka used to be considered the largest as well as the richest in the world; but probably they are equalled, if not surpassed, by those of Perak.

But another great source of revenue to the island of Banka is from the export of two kinds of timber, namely, Agila and Belian. Agila or eagle-wood (*Aquilaria agallocha*, L.) has been from time immemorial imported by the western nations from the East, and is supposed to be the "Aloes-wood" of Scripture. It is burnt like incense, but is also much used as the source of a perfume extracted from its resin. That exported from Banka is considered amongst the best. Belian (*Eusideroxylon zwageri*, T. and B.) is the iron-wood of commerce, belonging to the laurel family, and being found in abundance on this island, though it is also known from Sumatra and Borneo. I have seen trees likewise in the northern part of Celebes. The wood is of extraordinary hardness and durability, and is said to resist the white ant, which I question. At any rate it is considered a most valuable export, and adds much to the revenue of the island. The wood is exported in long beams, sawn to about 6 inches square. Muntok, the port of Banka, is opposite to the great alluvial delta of the Palembang river in Sumatra.

From Banka I proceeded to Bintang, the largest island of an archipelago between Singapore and Sumatra. It has an area of 3,336 geographical miles. It is a granitic formation with a low mountain chain like Banka, whose highest portion is only 1,368 feet above the level of the sea. On the western side, divided from Singapore by a narrow strait, is the Dutch settlement of Rhio whence twice a month steamers leave for Delli, the great tobacco district of central Sumatra. The geological formation is the same as Banka; but I am under the impression that there is a recent development of volcanic rocks which is not seen in other parts of the archipelago. It should be here mentioned that the so-called laterite formation gives rise to a fiery red soil, which is especially characteristic of these lands. The rocks are red, and so are all the roads of most parts of the Straits Settlements anywhere near the coast. This imparts great variety and brilliancy to the scenery.

STRAITS SETTLEMENTS.

From Bintang, the name of which in Malay signifies a star, I crossed to the Straits Settlements, remaining at Singapore for some time. During this period I went completely round the island, and in this and several other journeys made a more or less complete examination of its geology and that of the neighbouring state of Johore. The voyage round Singapore is one that can be easily made by steam in a few hours. It is an exceedingly picturesque journey through a narrow strait, bordered by low lands and rocky islands, varied in the most charming manner by the brilliant colours of the rocks already referred to. The vegetation even down to the water's edge is unusually luxuriant, either tropical jungle or plantations of coffee, cotton, tea, gambia and pepper, bordered by cocoa-nut and Betel-palms.

MALACCA.—In my first journey I left Singapore at the end of October 1883, and visited the ancient city of Malacca, a city which, even more than the well-known kingdom of Java, is connected with all the historical associations of the Indian Archipelago. The Portuguese, the Dutch and the English have all left amid the ruins of this curious eastern capital, some relics and memorials of their former history. Of the many churches, public buildings, monasteries and the large college, only one solitary ruin remains now, though heaps of stones and inscribed tombs, tell their own tales in quaint old Latin epitaphs, some nearly 300 years old. This is the scene of some of the most heroic labours of St. Francis

Xavier, and here his body for some short time found a sepulture. The old streets and suburbs of Malacca contain many an historic record. There is no place out of Java which so well repays attentive examination.

PENANG.—From Malacca I went to Penang, the seaport next in importance to Singapore and then the most northerly of the Straits Settlements. It is one of the most purely Chinese colonies, though the city and all its surroundings have been much modified by European, or say British, influence. Penang and the opposite province of Wellesly on the mainland are thriving colonies supporting a large population of industrious well-to-do people. I paid many visits to Penang in my journeys backwards and forwards. It was one of the central points of my travels to which I repeatedly returned. To the north of the province of Wellesly is the native state of Keddah, divided from the province by the river Salama. Twice I made boat expeditions up this river as far as Salama. This village may be called a Sumatran colony settled here for the purpose of mining for tin, which is very abundant. In one of my visits to this village I had the misfortune to witness the loss of a boatman's life through his having been carried off by a tiger.

PERAK.

After a short stay at Penang at the time of my first visit, I returned south to the native state of Perak, then under the administration of Sir Hugh Low. The port of entry was Matang, a low-lying mangrove swamp of the most unwholesome surroundings, and connected with the capital by a well-made road eight miles in length. Since that time, (1883) a railway connects the capital with Port Weld, a better harbour slightly nearer to Penang. Thaiping was then the capital, a Chinese mining town of about 10,000 inhabitants. It was well laid out in fine wide straight streets, in which the light sordid-looking bamboo shops and houses were rapidly being displaced by solid brick tenements. The old capital of Perak, or, at any rate, the residence of the rajahs was at the mouth of the Kangsa river at its junction with the river Perak. To this there was a good metalled road about 23 miles in length from Matang. This road was made through a low pass in a range of mountains running north and south, and dividing the valley of the Perak from the sea-coast. Kuala Kangsa was the residence of Sir Hugh Low.

I remained a longer time in the native state of Perak than in any other locality during the whole course of my travels; but I was not resident for more than a few weeks at a time, at each place. Thaiping was my central point, returning to and fro as each exploration was completed. When I say exploration, I do not mean the examination of places which Europeans had never visited before, for this did not often fall to my lot, but the geological and zoological exploration, as well as making botanical and zoological collections in nearly every place where I stayed.

It would be confusing if I were to attempt to follow a chronological order in the journeys made, so I must content myself with merely stating what were the places or districts visited in the course of my travels.

One of the first expeditions was in a large canoe down the river Perak, as far as its junction with the Kinta, and then, by means of this river, exploring much of the interior of the country drained by tributaries of the Perak. There is a range of mountains between the river Perak and the sea-coast, and both the range and the river pursue a nearly north and south direction. The eastern side of the valley of the Perak is a detached range of mountains, dividing the Kinta from the Perak; and where this range terminates to the southward the Kinta joins the Perak, and they form one stream for about 40 miles where the Perak discharges into the ocean. Almost opposite to its mouth is the group of islands known as the "Dindings," amidst which I remained dredging for some time.

I left my canoe at the junction of the Kinta, and proceeded up the latter river in a small steam-launch belonging to the Perak Government. This effected a great economy in time, as the usual mode of progression up rivers is by "poling," an exceedingly tedious method, which sometimes barely exceeds a mile an hour. My first resting place was at the old village of Kota Baru (New Fort), which was the central village of the district, and where the local magistrate or resident commissioner lives. The place, however, was nearly abandoned, owing to the floods in the river and the consequent prevalence of fever. A new settlement has since been formed at Batu Gadja, about six miles further up the river by land and 14 miles by water. From the new settlement Mr. Hewett, the local magistrate, sent a boat with four Malays, who in five hours poled us up to the station. The site of the town had just been cleared of jungle and was being surveyed. As an instance of the inconveniences to which Europeans are exposed, I may mention that the survey was being conducted by a gentleman who had brought his family with him. When the river overflowed everybody but himself got fever, and one of his daughters died. At the time of my visit there were 70 Chinese and Hindoo patients in the hospital of Kota Baru laid up with Beriberi fever. I am happy to add that the newly chosen station is much more healthy.

My journey from Batu Gadja was continued on elephants. The first stage was to Poussen mines, distant three and a half miles, where Malays were working shallow tin deposits. The tin occurred in an alluvial drift contained in pockets and pot-holes, in a much eroded crystalline limestone, which still retained traces of stratification. This limestone was either covered by a river gravel or cropped out in pinnacles and blocks. Here was also seen the only dyke of recent trap-rock observed by me in this part of the Malay Peninsula. At Pappan, four and a half miles from Batu Gadja, large tin mines were in operation, at least an opening was being made by a European company formed in Shanghai. The place had formerly been extensively mined by the Malays, and the former workings, now filled with water, bear curious testimony to the extensive nature of the deposit. Much of this country, extending over a large area, has been mined in former times by the Malays, and some of the operations date back to considerable antiquity. In the valley of the Kinta the country is singularly diversified by outcrops of crystalline limestone, which are outliers of an ancient formation, traces of which are found to extend through the whole of the Archipelago, and through Borneo and Palawan into the Philippine group. In the valley of the Perak there are also limestone outliers, but not so numerous. One notable precipitous hill, named Pondok, occurs in the pass between the sea coast and Kuala Kangsa. It is a gigantic rock of quite precipitous character, about 1,500 feet high. From Pappan I crossed a mountain track to Lahat, where the engineer and manager of a French mining company resided. He had cleared a small hill of jungle, from which a magnificent view could be obtained of the surrounding country. Ranges of mountains 5,000 to 9,000 feet high could be seen to the eastward, fronted by limestone hills 1,500 feet or so in height. From Lahat I crossed to the river Raya on elephants, partly through swamps, partly along the bed of a river, and partly through jungle. From this river a good open road enabled me to reach the village of Tecca, and then the extensive mining town of Goping. From this I returned to Kota Baru, and then in the steam-gig went down the Kinta to the Kampar River, along which I poled as far as the river Diepang, at the foot of the mountains. Here in precipitous limestone cliffs there were tin mines, worked in alluvial earth and limestone caves. This alluvium was some hundreds of feet above the present level of the valley, showing that there had been extensive denudation. This was my farthest point in the interior of the peninsula on the west side of the range, and from thence I proceeded down the river Perak to the Dindings. In all I travelled between 180 and 190 miles on the river Perak, the farthest north being at Enggor, an alluvial tin mine worked by Chinese, about eight miles up the river, and a little way back from the banks.

Besides these journeys through the tin mining district in the state of Perak, I remained on the mountains in different parts of the state, botanizing, collecting and making a series of observations connected with meteorology, heights of clouds, &c. The first of these stations was at Maxwell's Hill, as it is called, a sanatorium on the summit of a mountain only three miles in a straight line from Thaiping, but over three thousand feet above it. I remained about a month at this station. I subsequently removed to another mountain called Arang Para in the pass between Matang and Kuala Kangsa, and about the same height as Maxwell's Hill, but a better situation in many respects for observation. The bungalow is situated on the highest point of a spur, dependent upon a much higher mountain, namely Gunong Bubu, probably about 6,000 feet above the level of the sea. This mountain had never been visited by Europeans, being separated from the settled districts by several miles of dense jungle, and almost precipitous ridges and ravines. Assisted by Messrs. Bozzolo and Scortechini, I explored to the summit of this mountain, occupying myself in the examination of the country, and camping in the jungle for a couple of weeks. Several very interesting botanical and zoological observations resulted from this journey, not the least of which, was the discovery of a mountain flora similar to Mount Ophir in Malacca and some of the mountains of Borneo and Sumatra.

To the north of Thaiping along the coast in the direction of Province Wellesly, much of the alluvial flats and mangrove swamps has been reclaimed for the purpose of sugar-plantation. Some of these I also visited at the mouths of the rivers Krau, &c. The whole of the western coast-line of the state of Perak is almost entirely a low-lying mangrove shore, of very shallow muddy water, with dense jungle or lalung (*Imperata arundinacea*) scarcely raised above the level of the sea. Matang is at the mouth of the river Larut, and there are several other small rivers such as the Johore, the Limou, the Trong, &c. I visited many of these, as well as some of the long stretches of muddy islands which front the coast. To the south one river, a little longer than the rest, is called the Bruas. This river is mainly distinguished for the enormous number of crocodiles which it shelters. The mud is almost alive with them, and I have never seen such numbers, or such large crocodiles in any other place in the whole course of my travels.

SELANGORE, SUNGEI UJONG, &c.—Next to the state of Perak, to the northward is the state of Keddah, which was not under British protection at the time of my visit, but is a tributary of Siam. To the south of Perak is the native state of Selangore, an important territory which is under British protection. This state I visited and travelled through to some extent, but not so fully as the state of Perak. The Sultan of Selangore holds his court at Jugra, a native town with a thoroughly Malay agricultural population about it. The principal towns are in the mining districts on the river Klang; one being named after the river and was formerly the native capital, but is now far eclipsed by the centre of mining industry named Kuala Lumpor, which is the seat of British government and supports a numerous and wealthy Chinese population. The country around is singularly picturesque and beautiful, and this is owing to the extensive development of limestone formation which forms outliers on the granite. These are weathered into pinnacles and castellated outcrops like ruins of grand and varied shape. Within a few miles of Kuala Lumpor are limestone caves of large extent and magnificent beauty, from the colour and form of the stalactites. They form one of the most remarkable natural curiosities of the peninsula, though there are many other caves to be found in the limestone. To the south of the state of Selangore is that of Sungei Ujong which was a part of the territory I never visited. Beyond this was the state of Malacca, separated on the coast from Sungei Ujong by the river Linggi. I spent about six weeks in all, in the examination of the state of Malacca, living for a short time at several stations in the interior, as for instance at the hot springs (Ayer Panas) where the water bubbles out of the ground from the granite rock, at a temperature near to boiling, at Allor Gajah, where some 50 years ago we gained a victory over the Malays, at Gading where there are old tin mines, and finally I visited and examined the large mines at Chin-chin. The whole of this country is intersected by the most excellent roads, fit for any vehicle. Much of the north side of the state has been cleared of jungle and planted out by the Chinese in tapioca plantations or manihot, for which the ground is eminently fitted. Pepper, rice, and sago, besides much cultivated fruit are extensively produced. The state of Malacca is now principally dependent on its agriculture as it produces but little tin, and has no more than the name of producing gold. I have traversed its roads from Sungei Baru on the west to Sungei Kesang on the east, and from Malacca to Mount Ophir, and I found it, next to Java, the most civilized besides being the most picturesque part of the Indian Archipelago, but the scenery is of a subdued rural description compared with Perak.

PAHANG.—On the east side of the Malay Peninsula my travels were more restricted, for the states in this portion of Malaysia are poorly populated and but little known. One reason for this is that the eastern side is exposed to the full force of the monsoon for six months of the year, when it blows up the Gulf of Siam. Thus the mouths of the rivers emptying on the east coast become absolutely closed to navigation. Yet a special interest attaches to this portion of the continent, because some of the states have had a great reputation from time immemorial for the production of gold. The Spanish author Manuel Godinho de Eredia, writing in the commencement of the seventeenth century, speaks of gold dust found at Jelli in the kingdom of Pam. This is the river Jellis in the kingdom of Pahang, the state next to the north of Johore, on the east side of the peninsula and about 250 miles from Singapore.

Although so near to Singapore, it is surprising how little was known of the kingdom of Pahang. Probably not more than a dozen Europeans have visited it at various times. Of late years more keen attention has been paid to its rumours of mineral riches. About five years ago a government surveyor from Selangore undertook on his own responsibility and at his own expense the survey of the river Pahang; and this he accomplished in a singularly accurate manner, considering the means at his disposal. In 1884, the river was explored by Mr. Scaife, and early in 1885 Mr. Swettenham the Government Resident at Selangore crossed the range between Kuala Lumpor and the Jellis, while the year before

Mr. Scaife had crossed from the Semanten to Kuala Lumpor on foot and accompanied only by a few Malays. In July 1885, I proceeded from Singapore to the Pahang river in company with Mr. Scaife and a Mr. James. We intended to explore the river as far as the gold mines by means of a small steam launch belonging to the gold-mining company that was just formed. Our intention was also to report upon the mines which had been already explored by Mr. Scaife.

On entering the river Pahang we found the channel to be extremely tortuous and difficult. The town of Pekan which is the sultan's residence and the capital of the state.is about eight miles up the river. It is a large town with fewer Chinese inhabitants than is usual in these regions. Some of the houses are built upon rafts always floating in the river, but there is a good brick and stone mosque about the size of a small chapel. The sultan's palace is a more pretentious two-storied residence. In the centre of the town is a conspicuous shed, under which the principal nobility and government officers give all the vast resources of their intellects to top-spinning, often led by the sultan himself. The tops are the most effective things in tops outside of Japan, and in all the specialities and refinements of top-spinning they are second only to the Japanese. They can boast of having brought the industry to its highest degree of perfection, having spared nothing that labour or genius could bring to bear upon the subject. The importance of this speciality to the kingdom can be easily imagined.

As it was the fine season of the year, when the rains are comparatively light, the river was too low for our launch. Though only drawing three feet of water, we found it impossible to proceed, as we grounded almost every mile, even assisted by Malay pilots who knew the channel well. We lost more than three days in advancing about five miles. Then the sultan lent us a large canoe, with a crew of ten boatmen and a pilot. He also gave us a letter of recommendation to the different functionaries on the river, so that we could get help when we needed it. All these favours were only obtained after much delay, so that it was several days before we could make a start. The stream was too rapid and shallow to advance in any other way than by poling. It took us from the 27th July until the 6th of August to reach the gold-mines. At about 70 miles, we left the Pahang and ascended the Jellis, and at 60 or 70 miles further reached the gold mines which were carefully examined. I found them to be very rich and of great extent. Small quantities of gold dust were being continually collected by the Malay villagers from the refuse heaps by the side of the quartz reefs The appearances presented by the ancient workings were such, that I concluded that mining dated back for two or three centuries. Some of the marks of operations conducted there have a very ancient appearance.

Returning down the Jellis and Pahang to the junction of the Semanten I ascended the latter river for several days, reaching a few remote villages. I left the Semanten river at its junction with the Brentong—a river so much reduced and with such shallow rapids that this part of the journey was made in a small canoe. I ascended the Brentong as long as it was any way navigable, and having examined some poor tin deposits at the foot of the mountains, I returned down the river to Pekan, having been absent about six weeks, during the whole of which time, with the exception of one day, I was confined to the canoe. I found the Malays of Pahang to be a most interesting and simple race of people. They are agriculturalists, but extremely poor, so that we could scarcely obtain from them by purchase sufficient food for our wants. The coinage in use amongst them is small square pieces of tin. They are of the same form as those described by Tavernier, the French traveller, as having been in use in Keddah in 1677.* The details of my journey through Pahang are of the most interesting description, and I propose to give fuller details in a subsequent account which I hope to publish. Such collections as I was enabled to make confirmed what has already been partially known concerning the natural history of the country on the eastern

---

*Voyages de J. B. Tavernier, 2nd partie. Paris, 1677. Traité des monnaies des Indes.

side of the dividing range. The avi-fauna manifested a marked approach to that of China, and a slight variation from the Malayan sub-province of the oriental region.

The geology of the eastern side of the peninsula was also somewhat exceptional and remarkable. Instead of the universal prevalence of the granites and palæozoic schists, slates, and limestones of the western side of the divide, I found rather extensive outcrops of andesitic traps at about 70 miles from the coast, giving rise to subsidiary ranges of volcanic character and of moderate height; that is, from 1,500 to 2,000 feet. The physical features of the country were not only much modified by these ranges, but also, I believe, the flora and natural history as well. The gold mines were found to be geologically similar in age and character to those of Australia. The gold had been found originally in alluvial gravels, but latterly was derived from the breaking up and washing of large quartz reefs.

The flora did not differ materially from the general character of the Malayan vegetation, but the collections were not sufficiently extensive to determine whether there was a larger proportion of Chinese types than are usually met with on the west side of the divide. The species of forest trees, generally speaking, did not differ from those of Singapore, Malacca, &c, that is with a prevalence of fig-trees, *Dipterocarpus, Dryobalanops, Shorea, Hopea, Fagræa, Artocarpus, Eugenia, Jambosa, Sterculiads*, palms of the genera *Arenga, Licuala, Pinanga, Eugeissona, Borassus, Caryota, Areca*, and *Nipa*. Some of these are only cultivated. The river flora, moreover, seemed to be such as prevails throughout the whole Archipelago. The fresh-water mollusca differed but slightly from that of the western rivers. *Unio sub-trigonus* and *Unio delphinus* are as common in the river Pahang as at Malacca, and in both places are used considerably as articles of food by the natives.

BORNEO.

My travels in the Malay Peninsula had a long period of interruption in 1884, while I had the advantage of a cruise in Bornean and Sulu seas in one of Her Majesty's cruisers. It was thought desirable to collect accurate information for the Admiralty as to the various deposits of coal, of which there had been many discoveries in these islands. The acceptation of this commission gave me an opportunity which I had much desired of seeing the geology of this part of the Archipelago. I sailed in H.M.S. 'Pegasus' (Captain Bickford commanding), leaving Penang at the end of October. We passed close to Victory Island, a small peaked granite island about 150 miles from Singapore. On the third day also we passed the South Natuna Islands. Of these latter very little is known. They are inhabited by a peculiar Malayan people, or a mixture of Malay and Chinese, who are more than suspected of piracy when a chance offers. We were quite near enough to the land to see the houses and the clearings for cultivation, and even the men on the coral reefs spearing fish. There seemed to be a good deal of cultivation on the islands, which were prettily diversified with apparently volcanic peaks, and a dense tropical vegetation on some of the highest centres. The same evening we came in sight of the high land of Borneo.

LABUAN.—On the sixth day we reached Labuan, which had then a European population consisting of the Governor's family, the treasurer, and the gaoler with his family, in all about ten persons. At one time, when the coal mines were in operation, there was a larger population, but the mines have been abandoned for some years, and since then the place has been occupied by a small staff of government officials, a few Chinese merchants, and the Malay agriculturalists. The time of our arrival was somewhat opportune. The Sultan of Brunei had got himself into trouble with neighbouring tribes, who were killing his people under considerable provocation. He had asked the intervention of Governor Treacher, but while the Governor was trying to arrange with the Sultan's enemies, who were quite peaceably disposed, the Sultan treacherously incited the wild Dyaks (Muruts) to attack them, so that seven people were killed, and the Governor himself put in some peril. So glaring an insult could hardly be passed over, so that immediately after our arrival the Governor formally applied for the assistance of Captain Bickford in obtaining at least an apology.

BRUNEI.—Accordingly we sailed at once for Brunei, the mouth of which river is about 40 miles from Labuan. There all the ship's boats were manned and armed, and an expedition of about sixty blue-jackets under Captain Bickford, accompanied the Governor to demand some redress from the sultan. We found the mouth of the river almost blocked up by a kind of breakwater, by which the river was barred against the Spaniards a century or two ago. The sultan's people did not take our demonstration very seriously, for his prime minister sent his launch to meet us and to assist in towing the boats; but he had his revenge, for we slept on board this boat, and I have never, in the moderate experience of a lifetime, seen a steam launch infested with so many cockroaches. Our boots were nearly eaten off our feet.

It was somewhat interesting to be upon the river described so graphically by Pigafetta nearly 400 years ago. There has not been much change since then. The river is broad, with high ridges of serrated hills on each side, and villages built over water on high piles. But the city itself was just as Pigafetta saw it: a sort of bamboo Venice, the streets and squares, the courts and palaces were all built in the midst of the water without any means of approach except by boats. I suppose there is no city in the world so peculiarly constructed. The origin of this mode of residence doubtless arose from the bad habits of the Brunei people. They were in reality sea-gipsies who had given the inhabitants of the land so much reason for complaint that they could not trust themselves unreservedly on the shore.

The officers of the sultan gave a private audience to us on the evening of our visit, receiving us with what may have been intended as an honourable demonstration, but which looked like a reception by an armed rabble of very villainous-looking pirates. Every sort of excuse was invented to refuse the apology demanded. The next day the boats were brought up and the sultan admitted us to his august presence. The venerable potentate was 100 years old, and looked every hour of it. He was surrounded by an oriental court of truly theatrical splendour, presenting a scene of silks and satins, gold, silver, precious stones, feathers and tinsel unequalled anywhere. His Highness objected to make any reparation to the Governor, but the display of a little firmness by Captain Bickford induced him to say he would consider it. Captain Bickford said he would call again in three hours, and he departed leaving His Highness in some trepidation. Long before the three hours had elapsed, a royal embassy brought us a humble apology from the Sultan to the Governor expressing great regret for what had happened and promises of amendment for the future.

It need hardly be said that the journey to Brunei was replete with interest. It would take long to describe the interesting features of the people and their singular modes of living. My opportunities were but short, but still in that time I was able to obtain some information about the natural history which I hope one day to publish. On our return to the ship we made a special visit to a coal mine at the mouth of the river worked by two enterprising Scotchmen—Messrs. Cowie—on a mining lease granted by the Sultan. There is an immense outcrop of thick seams of tertiary coal, similar in age and appearance to the coal beds at Labuan, at Sarawak and the Dutch settlements on the south coast of Borneo. The mines are very interesting, being worked with the aid of Chinese coolies. Some trouble had been experienced from wandering tribes of Muruts at the time of our visit.

During our stay I also visited the old coal-workings at Labuan. There seems no scarcity of good coal which is going to decay, together with the valuable plant of machinery, pumping gear, tram-stock, loading and unloading pier, &c.

GAYA.—After leaving Brunei the 'Pegasus' sailed for Gaya about 90 miles further north where two Europeans, Messrs. Dalrymple and Little, represented the North Borneo Company, administering the government, collecting taxes, &c. This was one of the most interesting places that I saw in North Borneo. First of all the harbour was of great natural beauty, and not more than about 30 miles from the great Bornean mountain of Kina Balou. This is over 12,000 feet high and is a barren granite peak. The very high summits in the Archipelago are usually volcanic. The harbour is inhabited by Malay fishermen and a few Chinese storekeepers. The North Borneo Company have sago works, which were under the direction of the two European gentlemen already mentioned. The sago is obtained from the pith of the palm tree known as *Sagus lævis*. The material was bought from the natives. We then visited the bungalow which was up a steep hill about 400 feet high and commanding a lovely view. On our way we visited the prison and police station, situated half way up the hill and protected by a battery of four guns, manned by a corporal's guard of the North Borneo police force. In the prison were three head-hunters, wild Muruts, lately condemned for killing a poor Malay. One prisoner had a fearful half-healed gash over his head which his victim had given him. These wild men were of low stature, much fairer skinned than Malays, and of somewhat mild expression. They were quite naked except for a waist-cloth, the skin being slightly tattooed in very pretty coloured patterns.

While at Gaya we made an excursion into the interior among some of the agricultural Dusun tribes. We were six Europeans including three officers of the ship. We were carried across the bay in a small canoe, which was loaded to the water's edge by our large party and rendered very unsafe. Our course was then over some coral reefs between Gaya Island and the sea-shore, being exposed at one part to a considerable surf, which required watchful care to keep the canoe afloat. However, we got across without any other inconvenience than being scorched from the frightful glare and heat of the sun. After skirting along the coast for a few miles we entered the Besagas river, up which we rowed for a short distance until we came to a small Bajow or sea-gipsy village where we were provided with buffaloes to ride. It rained in heavy showers daily, and the country was quite inundated, with knee-deep water in places, and abounding with venomous snakes of small size, apparently of the genus *Bungarus*. The reptiles appeared to be too much absorbed in the capture of very pretty blue and green frogs, to do more than get out of the way of our buffaloes. We went across some fine rich plains, planted with paddy, all fenced and carefully tilled, as well as anything I have seen in the best parts of China. The beautiful green fields, with patches of jungle backed by the mountains towards which we were journeying, looked wonderfully picturesque. In a few miles we came to another village where we were welcomed by the inhabitants who offered us green cocoa-nuts. Beyond the village the Dusun country commenced. It was neatly tilled and had splendid crops all fenced in in the most orthodox fashion. It would be difficult to describe the extreme picturesqueness of the scenery which was almost European, from the evidences of careful husbandry on every side. The distant villages looked like farm-houses in some rural district. After passing a fine bungalow with an old orange and lemon orchard around it we came in a few miles to another village, which consisted of a house about 150 feet long, and a few other small houses. The style of this building was entirely of that Dyak pattern with which books of travel have rendered us all familiar. We entered it by climbing up a notched log, as it was raised on high piles. On either side was a long enclosed verandah which ran the whole length of the building. Inside the space was divided into dark apartments for each family. In the centre was a long beautifully matted room with a roof some 35 feet high. There we were welcomed by the chief of the village, who in this case was a female. She gave our party a warm welcome, and sent her people to cook rice for us. The central chamber was divided into two, and there were about 60 men, women, and children in each end. The cooking was performed on a small stone fireplace in the middle of the floor, and the smoke went up through the roof. The water and refuse went between the bamboos of the floor.

The Dusuns are not much burthened with clothing. What is wanting in drapery is made up with brass rings, coins, and coils of brass wire round the arms and legs. Nevertheless, they have more clothes than the Dyaks, and they have a modesty and reserve which would become a civilised people. They are not head-hunters except in retaliation, and it is seldom that strings of Murut heads are seen adorning their door-posts. The people bade us welcome, and gave us, after supper, a musical entertainment, in which a furious and unearthly din was performed by the whole strength of the company. After that there were war-dances and sham-fights unpleasantly like realities, making us almost wish to be on board the 'Pegasus' again. There was no word about going to sleep that night. The war-dance terminated about four in the morning, when the ladies gave a vocal performance, which was a very fair rendering of a 50-lb. steam-whistle. This lasted until it was time for us to go back to the boats, which we reached after a most fatiguing journey. This was due to the erratic proceedings of the buffaloes. They had taken an implacable dislike to their European riders, and continually interrupted their journey by senseless chargings at each other, which often unhorsed or unbuffaloed their burdens into the paddy swamps. I was never in any part of Borneo where finer collections of Dyak and Dusun war and domestic implements can be made. Some of the old Dyak warriors wear a coat of mail which reminds one of the armour worn by the old crusaders. I brought away many interesting specimens of swords, spears, and sumpitan tubes, which were of the finest description.

KUDAT.—From Gaya we proceeded to Kudat on the most northerly end of Borneo in Maruder Bay. Kudat is in the end of the bay where it is fringed by a coral reef. At the time of our visit there were half-a-dozen Europeans at the station which was at one time the head quarters of the North Borneo Company. The government bungalow is a large and more substantial building than usual. Kudat, however, has little or no fresh water. The rock is a carbonaceous sandstone with a steep dip inland. During our stay at Kudat we went in the government launch to the further side of the bay, on a deer-shooting expedition, which was not successful in the capture of much game but it afforded me a large botanical harvest. On returning at night-time we struck on the outer edge of a coral reef with a falling tide and a rising wind and sea with heavy rain. We remained all night in a most perilous position drenched with water and not without anxiety, as our only boat would not contain three persons. Fortunately we managed to get off the reef at high water next day, and succeeded in reaching Kudat without much difficulty. The population of Kudat reminded me much of that of the Philippines, and it was equally celebrated for cock-fighting.

From Kudat we went to Sandakkan now called Elopura, passing round the northern end of Borneo amid a downpour which exceeded anything I ever saw, in the way of rain. We could not see any distance ahead, and this part of our cruise was especially dangerous, being a perfect maze of coral reefs, which did not show above the water, and upon which there was no break. A narrow strait is formed between Borneo and Banguey and other islands to the north. These groups are mostly inhabited by sea-gipsies of ancient piratical fame. In some places the passage between the reefs is only a hundred yards or so wide. We were sometimes so close to the reefs as to be able to distinguish the coral and the shells, while the shouts between the navigating officer and the quarter-master, and the frequent stopping of the engines, made it exciting work. More than once we were about to anchor until the rain cleared. It was fine in the afternoon, revealing pretty scenery, and Mount Kina Balu showing well up in the south-east.

SANDAKKAN.—Early on the 12th of November we came to the opening of Sandakkan, which is extremely picturesque. On the north side are fine red sandstone cliffs, one 530 and the other over 600 feet high. Inside is the harbour, with a good wharf and many houses crowded round a small hill. At the back of this rise forest-clad hills about 800 feet high. Most of the houses are of native architecture and built on piles, but there were some striking instances of European influence in the better class of buildings, including some Chinese shops and an hotel. As we passed the sandstone cliffs we saw the base a good deal perforated by caves, into which some natives were entering for edible birds' nests; but much more valuable harvests of the same nests are gathered in enormous limestone caves about 18 miles distant from Sandakkan. In some of this limestone I found fragments of fossil *Fenestella, Stenopora*, &c. I take this opportunity of recording the extreme hospitality with which we were received at the North Borneo capital, where every one, from the Governor, Mr. Treacher, to the least official, tried to assist us in every way. I regret to add that many of those who welcomed us then have since perished. During my stay I went across to Bay Island, where I saw a large flotilla of about 50 canoes round a Bajow or sea-gipsy settlement, constructed upon piles far out in the water. I am afraid these Bajows would all be pirates if they dared. So the presence of the North Borneo settlement is of the utmost value to the safety of commerce, which is not the least service it renders to the Indian Archipelago. I visited a coffee estate and tobacco plantation at Suna Lamba, where a good crop of tobacco had been already obtained. I had rather unpleasant experience in returning at night, being overtaken by a violent storm, which exposed us to the wash of a cross sea for about three hours, and I considered myself fortunate to escape being swamped. We had been invited to dinner at Government House, but arrived instead at midnight drenched to the skin.

I saw at Sandakkan specimens of tin, gold, antimony, coal, and corundum. These had been obtained in an exploring expedition made by Mr. D. Daly up the Kinabatungan River. I have no doubt that considerable quantities of alluvial gold will be found eventually in North Borneo.

SULU.

From Sandakkan we proceeded to the Sulu Archipelago, which we reached in two days. On our way we passed the largest shoal of porpoises I ever saw. They were round the ship quite thickly as far as the eye could reach. We were passing through this shoal for many hours.

Sulu, or Suluk in Malay, is called by the Spaniards Jolo, the "j" being the Spanish guttural. The Sulu Archipelago extends from Cape Unsang, the most easterly point of Borneo, to Zamboanga, the most westerly port of Mindanao, or over 200 miles. The islands are volcanic, over 130 in number, but the majority too small to be inhabited. They are divided into seven groups—Sulu or Sug, which gives its name to the archipelago, Tawi-Tawi, and some others to be mentioned presently.

One peculiarity about the archipelago is that it is surrounded by an enclosed sea-basin of extraordinary depth, while the edge of this basin is a shallow sea of coral reefs. The different portions were visited by me on several occasions, and I had an ample opportunity for the examination of some of the least known portions of the group. It enabled me to conclude that the sea-bottom has subsided during the period of volcanic activity and this has probably happened in the seas round the most of the Philippine Archipelago. I believe I shall be able to show that the ancient prolongation of the Asiatic continent was extended not only through Borneo, but to some little distance north of the island of Palawan. The proof of this I shall mention in connection with the surveys of H.M.S. 'Flying Fish'

In Crawfurd's "Dictionary of the Indian Islands," there is a full description of these islands, which was all that was known about them in 1850. The great incorrectness of this account shows us how little that was. Mr. Crawfurd's information was mostly derived from Dalrymple.* Respecting its geology, he says we have little or no information, but it will be probably found to consist chiefly of sedimentary rocks, probably limestone and sandstone. This is incorrect as far as the greater number of

---

*Dalrymple, "Oriental Repertory." 2 vols. 8vo, 1793-1808. The author visited Sulu in 1759 and 1761.

these islands is concerned. They are, as already stated, volcanic. But if the geology is deficient, it is a matter of astonishment that Mr. Crawfurd was able to obtain so much information about the language and ethnography of the people.

The following is a description of the groups known to the Spaniards. (1) Balanguingui Group:—this group consists of fourteen islands, seven of which are uninhabited. In the rest the population is estimated by the mandarines, as the chiefs are called by the Spaniards, as capable of furnishing 325 men fit to bear arms. This is the peculiar way in which, in this region, information is furnished about the population. (2) Tapul Group:—21 islands, 10 uninhabited, 1,300 men of arms. (3) Group Keknaponsan:—eight islands, nearly all uninhabited, but furnishing 60 men of arms. (4) Group Tawi-Tawi, 42 islands, 30 uninhabited and 1,200 men of arms. (5) Tagbabas Group:—14 islands, none of which are inhabited. (6) Pangutaran Group:—23 islands, 12 of which are uninhabited, and in the rest 440 warriors. (7) Sulu Group:—13 islands, 7 of which are uninhabited: in the others 15,600 warriors, the greater part of whom live in Sulu. The Sulu Group is in every respect the most important of the whole. To this is added the Sulu-Cagayan island, which is widely separated from the rest, and is supposed to have about 400 warriors. This curious way of computing the population is derived from the unfailing war-like and piratical tendencies of the people. The whole number of the inhabitants, men, women, and children, including a large number of slaves is supposed to be about 20,000.

Some of the islands have mountains upon them of tolerable height. Thus Sulu, which is 34 miles long from east to west, has three parallel ranges from one coast to the other in an E.N.E. and W.S.W. direction. The principal summits are Tumantangis about 2,700 feet high, situated on the west, Tulipan on the southeast 1,900 feet high, and Mabustan about 1,300 feet. But the whole of the island is rugged and mountainous, with a width of about 12 miles and a circumference of over 100. It has about 30 towns and villages, the principal of which is Parang on the west with 3,000 inhabitants; Maibun on the south with 1,500, which is the residence of the sultan; and in the centre Siang with 800 inhabitants. The seat of the Spanish government is called by the name of the island and is on the north side. It is a very bad anchorage, the water being so deep that there are only one or two places where large vessels can be secured, and these unpleasantly near the shore.

All the towns in Sulu bear a family likeness to Brunei in Borneo. They are all built on the piratical lines of the Bajows or sea-gipsies, that is nearly wholly over the water on high bamboo stakes. The capital, as we may call Sulu, has a pretty appearance from the water's edge, with the usual Spanish campañero and small dome over the church. But Sulu is strictly speaking a military establishment. The military hospital lines the wharf, and the military barracks, with customs' departments of course, form the frontage of buildings, with large convict barracks as well. For it is also a convict establishment. Long-sentenced native prisoners are brought here from all the Philippines, but the poor easy-going Philippine Indian is not, even as a convict, a reprobate. The Spanish government reposes the highest confidence in him. On his arrival at Sulu he is put into uniform, supplied with an old percussion firelock, with a bayonet of soft and easy temper like his own, and thus more than 2,000 convicts co-operate as auxiliaries to the Spanish garrison. Beyond the military and prison establishments there are a few nice streets and squares passably built, and very tastefully adorned with gardens. Here, also, may be found a market, a few shops and some larger Chinese stores where the merchandise of pearls is carried on. Beyond this a strong wall of fortification completely encloses the place. Three miles further is a line of outposts, with towers of observation, for in fact the Spanish foothold is as yet only precarious and the place is held like a beleaguered city.

The history of the struggle between Spain and the Moros or pirates of Sulu dates back over 300 years, and until very lately the Moros had the best of it, and kept to their islands and their predatory habits. If Spain had had a good or strong government, or had not had its hands almost always full enough of sore troubles at home, it would have settled its accounts with this wasp's nest ages ago. At length, about 12 years back the matter was taken in hand in earnest, and the Spaniards got a foothold. They could not yet afford to despise their enemies however, who, to do them justice, left nothing untried in the way of treachery and savage warfare to make it hot for the Spaniards. At the time of my visit there was a temporary peace. Then came a disputed succession to the throne of the sultan, and a civil war. The Spaniards profited by the occasion nearly to "wipe out" the Sulu nation, and thus confer a lasting benefit on mankind.

During my stay at Sulu I had an interview with the sultan and his court, on the occasion of a visit from one of the rajahs of Palawan. He had come to visit the Spanish governor, and was accorded a public welcome. The peculiar splendour of a Malay court is easy to realise for those who are familiar with the etchings of books of travel in the East, of the last century. Theatrical spectacles and popular illustrations to the "Arabian Nights" will also give an idea of how silks and satins of rose, blue, and emerald green are mingled with tinsel and embroidery, shawls, scarves, and gems, to produce brilliant effects. His Highness of Sulu on this occasion had gorgeous rose satin tights, and was a mass of shawls round the waist, from which more than one jewelled *kris* peeped out. His turban was very brilliant, or, if you like, tawdry, and his whole make-up full of startling contrasts of colour. He of Palawan delighted in yellow satin tights, with other appurtenances which it would require a silk mercer to describe. Both these potentates were surrounded by a body-guard as varied in colours and as rich in materials as their masters, and they carried spears, knives and *krises* in threatening attitudes that were most objectionable on a peaceful mission, and calculated to distress timid people. Knowing the natural tendency of these pirates for impulsive assassination, I thought their whole bearing was treacherous and it made me feel uncomfortable. When they entered the town they were conducted to the central plaza, where chairs were provided, and we all sat in a circle while the band played, and played very nicely. It did not add to my enjoyment to find myself close to the sultan, behind whom stood a murderous-looking scoundrel in gorgeous livery, with a loaded revolver resting on his shoulder and his finger on the trigger.

The impressions I retain of Sulu are very scanty. In the market, and in the streets cock-fighting is much practised, and a man would as soon be seen without decent clothing as to appear in public without a game-cock under his arm. I remarked the same feature at Kudat in Borneo, but no place comes up to the Philippines in the matter of cock-fighting.

The island of Tataan, the principal of the group of Tawi-Tawi, is almost as large as Sulu. It lies about 30 miles south-east of the peninsula Unsang of Borneo. It rises to a height of about 1,500 feet, and is very rugged. The flora is rich, but the fauna is poor; and though the island is 40 miles long by 30 wide, it is scarcely inhabited.

The whole population are called Moors of Malay race. Those who live on the coast are called Samaluans, and those who live in the interior and are devoted to agriculture are called Guimbals. Between these two there exists a feud which is the cause of much strife and bloodshed.

The language of Sulu is peculiar. It belongs certainly to the Philippine dialects, and is also closely allied to the Malay. Like most of the Mahometan Malays the islanders write in Arabic characters. It may be said that they have two languages, one of which is pure Malay, and the other a dialect of Visayan, or more properly a language of the Philippine family, closely allied to the speech in use on the coast and river banks in Mindanao. It is stated confidently that the Sulu natives are Malays originally from Borneo, belonging to the Moros tribe called also Laununs. But this appears to be a corruption of the word Ilanon, a term at one time applied exclusively to the Malay tribes of the interior of the islands. The skulls that have been compared from Zamboanga and Sulu, have almost equal proportions. The cephalic index varies between 81 and 81·60. The skulls are decidedly brachycephalic, and are distinguished by the constant prominence of the frontal bone, and for their prognathism which reaches 69. The facial angle does not go beyond 84°, and frequently does not reach that. The cheek bones are not so widely separated as those of the Javanese, and this, combined with the low facial angle, inclines some ethnologists to establish analogies between the Moros and the aborigines of Sumatra. A study of the crania utterly destroys the hypothesis of an Arabian origin, which certain authors have ascribed to this race. The skulls of this people are widely distinguished from the handsome type of the Arab races.

The government of Sulu is an absolute despotism under a sultan, who now no longer refuses to call himself a vassal of the Spanish crown. Subordinate to the sultan the Moors are divided into a great number of tribes governed immediately by chiefs called datus. Slavery in its most objectionable form exists among the people. The children of slaves are slaves. Prisoners taken in war, and debtors who are not solvent, are slaves as well. The women are much given to steal each other's children and to sell them in other islands. In many other respects the law which obtains amongst them is the law of the strongest.

Agriculture is not much fostered. Some maize is grown, a little rice, sugar-cane and a number of roots such as sweet potatoes, yams, &c. Cocoa-nuts are abundant, with plantains, juanis, which is a mango of strong odour, mangosteens and many other fruits. Buffaloes and dairy cattle are used in tillage and as beasts of burden, but they have a splendid breed of ponies in the island. They have also many goats and Indian sheep. They are great bird-catchers amongst the white cockatoos, pigeons and other birds. But their principal industry, besides piracy and robbery, is the pearl fishery, which is conducted by divers on the edges of coral reefs and on certain beds of the pearl-oyster which abound round Sulu. The people also are clever in making weapons and giving a fine temper to steel weapons. They manufacture their own krises, swords, lances, &c., and they cast their own cannon in bronze.

Most writers have called attention to the singular influence which Sulu has obtained over the other islands. Not only its influence, but its power and civilisation far exceed that of the other islands, and have enabled the sultan to extend his authority over them and over Palawan, and at one time also over several parts of Borneo and the adjacent islands.

CAGAYANES GROUP.

The Cagayanes Islands, though 130 miles to the north, are included in the Sulu group. I visited these in H.M.S. 'Flying Fish' when we were employed in searching for certain shoals that had been reported in the neighbourhood. The group lies 21 leagues to the westward of Negros Island in the Philippines.

Bounding the west side of the strait are two low woody islands of considerable size. The largest is to the westward, and is filled with islets and rocks. They are surrounded by a reef which projects to the northward. To the south-west, 10 miles distant, are a few small rocks called Cabesa, and at 26 miles a group called Cavili.

Cavili or Caueli is a high sandbank with a belt of trees, the breakers extending nine miles from its south-west side. This makes the islands particularly dangerous, because they are almost invisible from where the reefs begin. The island is wooded with heavy timber, and is surrounded for three-quarters of a mile with a fringing coral reef. The breakers mentioned above are on a detached reef, having on it a small sandbank or cay with trees. In other parts, also, the sand is dry, of an oval shape, the greater length being in a north-east and south-west direction, and in size similar to Cavili. When the Cagayanes Islands bore west by north about 18 miles distant, they were just visible from the deck. The body of them is in lat. 9° 34' N., long. 121° 17' 30" E. There is an opening in the reef off the south point of the most easterly island, with soundings of four or five fathoms inside, forming a kind of harbour for small vessels.

During our stay at Cagayanes we were generally anchored so far from the little harbour just mentioned that it was not easy to make an expedition to the islands. Once or twice we attempted it in the ship's cutter, but were obliged to return, as the time at our disposal was not sufficient in the state of the weather. All we could do was to land upon some of the sandbanks or cays, where an immense number of boobies had made their nests. Here, also, great flocks of halcyons or frigate-birds were hovering, and waited each evening for the returning boobies with their provender of fishes to feed their young. The plundering of the poor boobies has often been described by various naturalists from the times of Basil Hall to our own day. We used to witness it every night from our anchorage. It is not without amusement that one sees the weaker bird made to disgorge the result of his day's fishing, which, as it falls, the frigate bird catches with a swoop ere it reaches the water. In spite of it all the young birds dont do badly, though they abound in the low stunted brushwood which grows on the cays. The vegetation was of the usual kind found on all coral islands from Australia to Singapore, such as *Terminalia, Scævola, Cordia, Barringtonia*, &c., &c.

Admiral Belcher of H.M.S. 'Samarang' visited the Cagayanes in 1845. He says, "Effected a landing on a small rocky island in the channel between the two largest islands. A rapid survey was made during our detention of six hours. Found three more islands and very extensive reefs extending as far as the eye could reach, from our most elevated situation about 100 feet above the level of the sea. The islets are upon the outlines of the northern reefs, the most distant about 10 miles. Visited by a boat from the pueblo, which was pretty large and contained a whitewashed fort and church. We had not time to examine it; but one of the authorities deputed to make inquiries about us, and who endeavoured to make himself understood in a jargon of Spanish, Malay and Visayan, assured me that everything I inquired for (bullocks, vegetables and fowls) could be procured at the pueblo. From the tenor of their inquiries, I was led to infer that whale-ships touched here for water and refreshments. The bays and creeks in the interior of the extensive sound formed by the two greater islands are very picturesque, and have at their entrance or chord of the bay a depth of not less than 3¼ fathoms."

COCHIN CHINA.

I visited the port of Saigon in the course of my travels on my way from Hong Kong to the Malay kingdom of Pahang. It takes but three days to go from Singapore to Saigon, passing by Pulo-Condor, the Malay name for the island of reptiles, which is inhabited by a population of about 300 islanders. The entrance to Saigon is by the Cocoa-nut Bay and then up one of the many branches of the river Me-Kong, which flows through the delta of Cochin China. The time of my visit was unfortunate, for the Tonquinese war was going on, and cholera was causing great ravages amongst the people. The establishment of the French Messageries is at an angle of the river just at the entrance of the town of Saigon. All along the sides of the river crowds of sampans and canoes remind one of Hong Kong, though not nearly so numerous. There is a certain floating population here as in all China. There are families living continually on the water, eating, cooking and sleeping in a space incredibly small, while the infants are cradled in a swinging cot like an aerial plant, with no trouble in rocking. At night there is the usual sparkling of light and tinkling of sounds from the flotilla with its living freight.

There is nothing to be seen in coming up the river, except the low banks at either side, until one comes in sight of Saigon. This is only indicated by the two tall square towers of the cathedral and a forest of masts and steam-funnels above the wide brown dead level plains. We did not pass many boats except a few fishermen in vessels rigged like the feluccas of the Mediterranean. A few low attap or palm-leaf houses may have been indications of villages. The people looked like Malays, and, except that they are slighter in stature and have smaller features, reminded me very much of the Javanese. They are not like Chinese, and they do not wear the queue. The women wear long loose dresses of blue or white material, and over this a long dark blue robe like a soutanne. This, with a large silver ring round the neck and a good many pins in the hair, completes the costume. There is little difference between the male and female costumes, except that the men commonly wear something on their heads with combs of tortoise-shell and silver. The general aspect of the people is prepossessing, with a more amiable manner than the Chinese, combined with much modesty and decorum.

SAIGON.—The wharf at the Messageries is prettily shrouded at its termination with clusters of mango, tamarind and cassia trees. There is about half-a-mile of road from this through swampy plains into the town, but one can enter it in a shorter way by crossing the elbow of the river in a boat. The town itself is thoroughly French, and, but for the motley suits of the inhabitants and the luxuriant trees which fringe the pathways, one could well imagine oneself on the outskirts of Marseilles, or some French town on the Mediterranean. The streets are wide and regular, with unceasing groves of tamarind trees. The cafés are numerous, with a homely array of benches and tables extending into the streets, round which there are always crowds of soldiers and officers gathered. Whatever business is done is almost confined to the Chinese, who have most of the large shops and stores in their hands. Apart from the military, there cannot be much European population, but there are a few shops or *magasins* of the usual French type. However, a walk through the town of Saigon does not take very long, and whatever there is to be seen is soon disposed of.

About two miles out of town are the Botanic Gardens, which, though only in their beginning, are as good as anything that can be seen in the East; but one cannot walk far without coming upon some of the unreclaimed portions, and this for the present mars the effect. The zoological collection is very good, with two of the largest tigers I have seen anywhere. In a country where the plumage of the birds is in perfect harmony with the luxuriant foliage and the flowers, a large aviary well kept and tastefully arranged is a beautiful sight worthy of the famed splendour of the East.

At a short distance from the gardens, in a rather dreary-looking plain and surrounded by large military barracks, is the cathedral. It is a stately and imposing-looking building, even though it is stuccoed and coloured with yellow limewash. One cannot help being struck with the facts that this cathedral represents. The stately pile dedicated to St. Francis Xavier, the patron of missions, stands on a spot where a few years ago the brave missionary had to hide amongst a few fishermen's huts, and baptized his converts at the imminent peril of his life and theirs. There have not been wanting in Saigon many illustrious apostles, who laid down their lives in testimony of the truths they preached. And now the seed has produced its fruit, and the religion of the martyrs is the dominant one at Saigon. Unhappily there has been a conquest by the French flag as well as by the cross. The case may have been one where the force of circumstances produces events which no one could control; still all friends of the true interests of Christianity must wish that the territorial conquest and the work of the missionary had been kept entirely apart.

With cholera and small-pox all around, and the city full of sick patients invalided from the seat of war, and with the war itself going on, not without disaster to the French arms, it may be guessed that Saigon was not the most agreeable sojourn for a tourist.

There are a number of little villages in the plains outside Saigon. The native houses are much in the Malay style, with the usual shelter of tropical fruit trees and a formidable hedge of bristling cactus. During the dry season there are some pretty promenades amongst the Anamite villages. A much-frequented excursion is to the tomb of the Bishop d'Adran. Besides this the principal journeys for tourists are to the town of Cholen, "Les Jardins des Mares," the stand, the rifle butts, &c.

Two roads lead to the tomb of the Bishop d'Adran: that of the third bridge is the most picturesque, passing before the government offices, the native camp, and the place where formerly the literary examinations used to be held. It was there that, on the 5th of April, 1862, the treaty of peace between France, Spain, and Anam was signed. At present it is a barrack for the marines. Leaving to the right the rich village of Go-vap, one meets a succession of farms for the cultivation of tobacco, pea-nuts, and the fruits and vegetables which supply Saigon. Amidst these there are remarkable tombs under handsome groves of mango trees and sugar palms. The track is hardly practicable except on horseback, but by the village of Thuan-keou vehicles go right up to the tomb.

On leaving Saigon one sees the pagoda of Barbet, so called after a captain of marines who here fell into an Anamite ambuscade and lost his life. Here also King Minh-mang was born in 1789, and in memory of this event his father, King Gial-Ong, raised this pagoda, giving it an Anamite name, which signifies "The Aurora of Promise." At present the pagoda and its dependencies are used as a colonial state school.

This road crosses the Plain of Tombs, an immense cemetery, which proves that Saigon has long possessed a considerable population. The appearance of these tombs is very peculiar. They are occasionally little pyramids with a square or hexagonal base, or small pagodas in miniature, with doors "arch in arch," and guarded by stone dragons. More commonly they are square graves scattered without order on an arid, dusty plain, which boasts only of an occasional clump of trees. This is the aspect of the country which extends from Saigon to the Chinese town of Cholen and the lines of the Ki-hoa.

After having crossed the moat one sees the traces of defences constructed by the Anamites at this point, for it was here that the most desperate struggle took place of all the battles of the war of Cochin China. It resulted in the taking of the works by Admiral Charner in 1861. Here Col. Testard and Lieut. Larégnère were killed. A monument in marble has been raised to the memory of the latter officer at the place where he fell. Close by is a grand grove of mango trees, and it is here that the Bishop d'Adran dwelt, and he it was who introduced mangoes into the country. The name of this prelate was Monseigneur Pigneau de Behaine. He was born at the town of Aurigny, near Laon, and was Vicar Apostolic. It was through his efforts that a treaty was concluded in 1787 between Louis XVI. and King Gial-Ong. This treaty would have been of the greatest use to France if the ill-will of the French governor of Pondicherry and the confusion of the revolution of 1789 had not interfered with its good effects. The French say the Bishop d'Adran rendered the greatest services to King Gial-Ong, or Nguyen-Anh, for he had both names. The benefits derived from these services have proved somewhat equivocal, for they have led to the annexation of the country. However, they subdued the king's enemies for the time being; and as soon as he was peacefully established on his throne, Bishop d'Adran retired to the garden that he possessed near Saigon. He died 9th October, 1799, and the king gave him a magnificent funeral. He raised over his remains a monument in the style of an Anamite pagoda. Within this is an altar on which one sees the double blazon of the episcopal see and the arms of Monseigneur d'Adran, on whom the king of France had conferred the title of Count. Opposite the tomb is a stone covered with Chinese inscriptions. The whole is surrounded with an encircling wall, ornamented with the conventional animals such as the Cochin Chinese delight to put around their graves. This tomb has always been respected even when the Anamite troops occupied the plain of Ki-Hoa.

CHOLEN.—Every one who visits Saigon goes to see Cholen, which is five or six kilometres distant. Boats go every half-hour, and the passage is a most picturesque one. There is also a railway of modest pretensions, which passes along the roadside, leaving to the left the pretty village of Choquan, and in five kilometres one arrives at Cholen. The entrance is in front of the public offices of the paymaster, the prefecture, the telegraph office, barracks for the French garrison, and many pagodas, amongst which is the pagoda of the warrior gods. On the principal altar is an idol with a white beard having in his hands a bow and arrows. This is probably Kouang-Ti, the Chinese Mars; his son Kouang-Ping and his faithful esquire are at his sides. There is also the temple of Kwan-Chin Whay-Quan, erected by the Chinese of Canton to the goddess Koang-Yn or Apho, the creative power, the mother of the Chinese of Canton, the patroness of navigators and the Chinese Amphitrite.

The town of Cholen has a population of 10,500 Chinese, 32,000 Anamites, besides a floating population of 8,000, which gives a total of about 50,000 souls. It may be here mentioned that though Cholen is the head-quarters of the Chinese, they are pretty well scattered also throughout Cambodia. The first extensive arrival of Chinese took place about 1680, in the west of Cochin China, and was from Canton. A part was established at Bien-hoa, and a part at Mitho. This immigration was followed by many others coming from Fokien and other Chinese provinces. The superiority of their civilization and their wonderful aptitude and talents for trade, their spirit of association, their community of religion and customs, and of writing with the Anamites gave to the Chinese a great footing in the country. After the war between the rebels of Tay-Son and King Gial-Ong, they quitted their first establishments and came to dwell in Cholen about 1778. Although in 1721 the chief of the Tay-Son rebels had massacred more than 10,000 Chinese, and pillaged their stores, yet they continued to progress. Notwithstanding nine months of frightful famine in 1802, notwithstanding the prohibition to export any produce from the country, the perseverance of the Chinese surmounted every obstacle, and in 1830 Cholen was already a market of great importance, which the Chinese had named Taingon, and the Anamites Sai-gon. The only name now in use for the town is Cholen, Cho meaning market and lon, great. The Chinese are principally aggregated together in hongs or corporations. The chiefs of these congregations are responsible for their members as in Java.

The Chinese generally marry Anamite women. They have very pretty children, and the mixed race forms a very intelligent class amongst the natives, which is named Minh-huong. These half-castes are generally well off.

The town is divided into five quarters, each having a Chinese chief, a Minh-huong chief, and an Anamite chief. It is found to be very necessary to oblige the Anamites to take part in public institutions, as they are by nature indolent and retiring, or apathetic to a pernicious extent. The town has quite a European aspect: the streets are large; there is a canal with wide quays on each side. Amidst these quays are crocodile parks where these saurians are preserved and fattened for eating. The houses and shops are well built, and the whole place has an astonishing air of industry and prosperity, which reminded me of Penang or some of the best Chinese towns in Java.

About a quarter of an hour's walk from Cholen, on the road to Mitho, is the garden of Cay-mai. In a delicious situation on an artificial mound the Cay-mai tree grows, whose sweet-smelling flowers were offered to the Emperor to flavour his tea. It was death to touch them in former times. From this point the view extends over the ricefields which line the commercial canal, over the Plain of Tombs, the mines of Ki-hoa, the fields and the woods of Go-Vap as far as the mountain of Tai-Minh, a distance of nearly 100 miles.

It must be understood that it is only the lower part of the delta of the Me-kong that is called Cochin China. The upper portion of the river to the north-west is occupied by the kingdom of Cambodia. To the north-east is the kingdom of Anam. The boundaries of French Cochin China are between 10° and 11° N. lat.

One sees but few Cambodians at Saigon. They are easily recognised by their short hair, their shovel hats, and their dress. They are more robust and taller than the Anamites. They wear a loose robe with a little vest buttoned in front and a cincture of silk. Often they have only a piece of calico over the shoulders. Some come by boats from higher Cambodia to bring their produce to Cholen. Others come from the lower Anamite provinces, and others from the right bank of the great river by the route of Trambang, and bring herds of cattle and sheep.

The French have established schools in Saigon and Cholen, which are eagerly made use of by the Chinese and Minh-huongs. The Anamite character is the Chinese a little modified. It is at once ideographic and phonetic, so that they have no difficulty in writing European words. A Chinese not knowing the Anamite language can make himself understood by the characters which, though quite different to him in sound and pronunciation, represent the same ideas in the two countries. All official documents are written in Chinese.

There are two native newspapers, the Gia-dinh-bao, a gazette printed in European characters, and another journal, Nhut-Khim-Nam-Ky, which means the journal of Cochin China. The Anamite language is intoned, and it has six tones, like the Chinese; the same word having, according to the tone, many significations. It is extremely difficult to Europeans. The whole time at school is taken up by the natives in learning the characters. It takes years to be able to read a book. The best books to consult for this study are the Latin-Anamite dictionary of Mgr. Taberd, of which M. Aubaret has edited a French-Anamite edition; the dictionary of Père Le Grand de la Liraye; the grammar of Père Fontaine, and the vocabulary of Peter Ky. Like the *Pigeon-English* of Hong Kong, Cochin China boasts of a Pigeon called Sabier, a word of Portuguese origin. It is a mixture of Chinese, Portuguese, English, French, Spanish, Latin and Anamite. A specimen will suffice. Look, sir. Tou tou or, choum-choum, and so forth.

I conclude this short notice of Cochin China by saying that the people seem contented and happy, and the country progressing. The only persons who seemed wofully out of sorts were the French themselves. One soon becomes convinced that this colony has become painfully oppressive to the French nation. First of all, Cochin China is far from France; the climate is difficult to bear for any length of time; the French do not want to emigrate; the land is in the hands of natives, who are cultivators; the industrial uses of products are in the hands of Chinese, who have all the capital. The poor Frenchman shrugs his shoulders and says that this is not a country to organise or to colonise. The mission of civilisation has hitherto unfortunately demanded much gunpowder and bayonet; and, besides the military, the colony only gives support to about 400 unhappy French people, who one and all continually bewail their exile.

While in Cochin China I found the work of Chas. Lemire, entitled "Cochin Chine Française" (Paris, Challomel, 1884), a most useful guide, and it is to its pages many of the foregoing statements are due.

HONG KONG.

I first visited the south Chinese coast in 1885, arriving at Hong Kong in the middle of January, or, as I may call it, the depth of winter. It was piercingly cold at the time. All the inhabitants who could afford them were wrapped up in winter furs. The air was cloudy, damp, gloomy and raw to an extent which recalled to my mind the melancholy fogs of London. Having come straight from the fervid temperature of Singapore, the change can be imagined. Three days after leaving the Straits all our Chinese passengers came on deck swathed to the eyes in quilted silks or cottons. It was evident that we were in a new region. We were passing many fishing junks of the unmistakable Chinese pattern: the sails of palm canvas, with bamboo laths across them like Venetian blinds. These junks, with thin radiating ribbed sails, apparently lop-sided and conspicuously down by the head, are characteristic sights to be seen nowhere but in China. In their marine architecture, as in everything else, the Chinese keep distinct from all the world.

Amid the fog and mist which came thickly down upon us, we steamed amongst many barren-looking granite islands, about the fifth day from Singapore. At last one island with a very high peak upon it, loomed out from the clouds at no great distance, soon near enough to discern the forests of masts and crowds of steam-funnels, junks, sampans, and small steam launches which told unmistakably of a large seaport. As we neared it in the dull light of that cold foggy day, it looked as picturesque as any place I have ever seen. It may be defined as thick rows of masts; then handsome terraces of houses rising tier above tier upon such a steep incline that they looked as if each higher range were founded on the chimney-pots of the other. About half-way up the houses ceased, and then diagonal and zig-zag roadways, with scattered villas rapidly ascended into the clouds. A piercing cold Siberian wind was blowing keenly upon the animated scene of great rafts of steamers loading and unloading, a goodly fleet of men-of-war, and, as we neared the wharf, excited, surging, shouting crowds at the water-side. Hong Kong has often been described, but its wonderful population must be seen to be understood. Enormous crowds of boat-women, junk sailors, and coolies, which make a living stream on the quay, have no parallel in Europe or Asia.

Certainly Hong Kong is not a Chinese town, but a town for Chinese, but yet not of European architecture, nor like the Straits Settlements. Its crowded by-streets and lanes, the absence of horse-carriages, the presence of chairs and jinrickshas make it very peculiar. There are plenty of soldiers in red coats and plenty of sailors in naval uniform, and all sorts of picturesque Chinese costumes, a few Hindoos and Malays, besides Parsees of portly presence and European dress surmounted with a hat like a stove-pipe.

I am not going to describe any more of Hong Kong. I believe it is the most hospitable town in the East, almost surpassing the Straits Settlements and Shanghai. The merchant princes live in real splendour, extravagant if you will, but really comfortable. In winter sporting, hunting and other such amusements are out of the question; but for cricket, lawn-tennis, foot-ball and such like, and for balls, parties, private theatricals, &c., it is the gayest of gay cities. Yet I am told that the officers of the army and navy do not care much about being quartered at Hong Kong. Even gaiety becomes monotonous on an island scarcely nine miles long, so rocky that you cannot ride, and where pirates and squalls keep people from boating or fishing.

The island formerly constituted a part of the district Sun-on. It is scarcely a mile from Kiu Lung or Kow Loon on the main land, which is also British property. It is mainly granitic, but with a varied geology, so as to make it a most interesting place of study. There are some volcanic dykes in places, and traces of minerals, especially lead and molybdenum, of which fine specimens may easily be obtained. The highest peak is 1,825 feet high, and there are other peaks ranging between that height and 1,000 feet. Hong Kong as far back as the Ming dynasty belonged to the Tang family, whom I suppose everybody knows. It is an island at the mouth of the Canton river, and was a noted resort for pirates, who used to lie in wait for sailing craft in the Ly-ee-mun pass, a very narrow strait between the mainland and the island. In January, 1841, it was ceded to Great Britain. The capital is called Victoria.

VEGETATION.—It is an exceedingly picturesque island with a coast indented by several deep inlets, with bold headlands, broad sandy beaches and precipitous cliffs, giving rise to beautiful varieties of scenery. The surface soil is poor and stony, and for the most part with a poor heath-like flora, barren and bleak in the extreme. The more sheltered valleys and ravines sustain trees of stunted growth, consisting of few species such as *Pinus sinensis*, *Ternstræmia japonica*, eight small species of oaks and some others.

The greatest interest was attached to the knowledge of the Hong Kong flora; it was, so to speak, our first insight into the botany of China. Small contributions to its knowledge were made by Messrs. Hines, Champion, Hooker, Hance, Harland, Wright, Eyre, Wilford, &c., but the complete enumeration of the flora was not made until G. Bentham published his list in 1861. This included 1,056 species, distributed into 591 genera and 125 orders. More than ten years afterwards, a supplement was published by Dr. H. F. Hance, who added 73 new species and distinguished a few more which had been included by Bentham in other genera or species. This very large total amount found upon so small an island is wonderfully interesting. Another noticeable feature in this large census is the tropical character of the great majority of species, though the general aspect presents features of much more northerly latitudes. Though the more sheltered valleys and ravines on the northern and western sides are saturated with moisture during the long-continued rains of spring and summer, yet the temperature and degree of humidity are very variable.

As the island is exposed also to the burning heats of a tropical sun, and frequently the cold devastating fury of a Chinese typhoon the average range of the thermometer is between 45° and 100° of temperature, but greater extremes of cold are occasionally felt. Another peculiarity of the flora is the large proportion of arborescent and shrubby species on a rocky mass, where woods are limited to a few ravines or short, narrow, half-cultivated valleys. Other exceptional features may be enumerated as follows. First, there is a very great diversity amongst the species themselves. Secondly, as a consequence of the former feature there is a notably excessive proportion of orders and genera to species. Thirdly, there is a considerable number of monotypic genera which, according to Mr. Bentham, is far larger than that of any other flora known to him. Lastly, there is a very large number of endemic species not known to exist outside the island, though probably their range will be found to be greater when the flora of China is better known.

Out of the thousand and odd species belonging to the flora, it must be said that 100 of them are weeds which follow cultivation, or plants cultivated in spite of man. The greater part of these are indigenous to tropical Asia, with a dozen European strangers, and half that number from America.

The Hong Kong flora has little resemblance to the American, but there is a strip of American plants found in Japan, and gradually falling away through Manchooria in Central Asia, though a few are found as far as the Himalayas. This flora passes to the north of Hong Kong, though it has a few representatives such as *Lespedeza, Solidago, Eupatorium, Olea marginata, Gelsemium,* &c., the other American plants found in Hong Kong are such as are diffused through tropical Asia generally. One stranger (*Teucrium inflatum,* Sw.) makes its way to the island through the South Pacific Islands.

With Australia the flora of Hong Kong has a small connection, but mostly in insignificant herbs, maritime plants, grasses, and sedges, some of which are of wide range; while others, such as *Stylidium, Mitrasacme, Thysanotus, Philydrum,* are characteristically Australian.

The general character of the Hong Kong flora is that of tropical Asia, but many of the species attain their northern limit in the island. The flora of the damp wooded ravines contains some species of north-east India, such as Khasia, Assam, and Sikkim. Others have a much more tropical character, extending with little variation over the Indian Archipelago, the Malay Peninsula, and even to Ceylon and tropical Africa. Northwards of Hong Kong the tropical character of the vegetation changes rapidly. This is seen in a remarkable manner in the relations of the flora to that of Japan. A number of Japanese species range across to the Himalayas. But they come no further south than Amoy. This port is only two degrees north of Hong Kong, yet there the tropical character of the flora has entirely disappeared. There are, however, some characteristic Japanese plants to be found in Hong Kong, such as *Kadsura* (Magnoliaceæ), *Stauntonia, Actinidia, Camellia, Eriobotrya, Distylium, Benthamia* (not extending further south or west), *Farfugium* (cultivated in Loo Choo and Japan), and *Houttuynia*.

About 150 species are supposed to be endemic, but one reason for this is the wholesale destruction of every kind of plant which goes on upon the mainland. The people being destitute of fuel burn everything, even to the roots of the grasses. This gives a tanned and barren appearance to the land in most places, which is very desolate, and, united to the dilapidated and sordid aspect of all Chinese houses, makes the scenery in South China dreary in the extreme.

The orders most numerous in Hong Kong are as follows:— Gramineæ, 86 species; Filices, 75; Leguminosæ, 72; Compositæ, 67; Cyperaceæ, 62; Euphorbiaceæ, 52; Rubiaceæ, 42; Orchideæ, 36; Urticaceæ, 27; Scrophularineæ, 21; Acanthaceæ, 18; Verbenaceæ, 17; Labiatæ, 16; Myrsinaceæ, 15; Laurineæ, 14; Apocynaceæ, 13; Convolvulaceæ, 13; Ternstrœmiaceæ, 12; Malvaceæ, 12; Rosaceæ, 11; Asclepiadeæ, 11; Solanaceæ, 10; Polygonaceæ, 10; Amentaceæ, 10.

The above will give a good idea of the general character of the flora.

The genera most numerous in species are, exclusive of the cryptogams, as follows:—*Panicum*, 16; *Ficus*, 15; *Fimbristylis*, 13; *Cyperus*, 12; *Quercus*, 10; *Polygonum*, 9; *Carex*, 9; *Eragrostis*, 9; *Desmodium*, 8; *Phyllanthus*, 8. Five genera have seven species each, 10 have six, seven have five, 14 have four, 43 have three, 91 have two, and no less than 408 genera have but one species each. This large disproportion of the small genera is one that frequently meets us in floras which are on the borders of several botanical provinces. The cryptogamic flora is not so well known. Like all moist climates the ferns are numerous and beautiful, including 13 species of *Aspidium* and 10 of *Asplenium*. The ornamental drooping fronds, on every wall and terrace, of *Pteris cretica*, *P. longifolia*, *Gleichenia dichotoma*, *Adiantum lunulatum*, and *A. cordatum*, make the moss-grown walls of Hong Kong a mass of the prettiest vegetation. The indigenous and introduced ferns of the island have been made the greatest use of for ornamental purposes in the lovely shady walks in and about the city and suburbs of Victoria.

The moss flora of Hong Kong does not appear, according to Dr. Hance, to be at all rich. He gives a list of 20 species recognised up to 1872.

Some of the remarkable features of the flora of Hong Kong may be summed up as follows:—*Rhodoleia championi* is a beautiful small tree found only in the island, resembling camellia, while the bright pink petals of the five or six flowers of the head are arranged camellia-like. *Camellia hongkongensis* is another floral beauty of the island. The hillsides are likewise covered with bushes of *Rhodomyrtus tomentosa* with large pink flowers. *Enkyanthus quinqueflorus* is an elegant shrub with showy red flowers tipped with white. Probably this is the only species known of the genus. *Melastoma repens*, *M. macrocarpon*, and *M. decemfidum* are three very pretty members of the genus, which cover the hillside with pink flowers nearly all the year round. *Ipomœa tuberculata* is also spread more or less over the island, flowering during the whole year. Dr. Hance says no plant grows so rapidly and spreads over such an enormous space, while it twines so as to kill many trees and shrubs. The old stems are so tenacious as to make admirable ropes. The arborescent, flora, besides the oaks and fig-trees already enumerated, includes a beautiful chestnut tree, the white-stemmed *Liquidambar, Altingia chinensis*, and *Styrax odoratissima*, with most fragrant racemes of flowers like white lilac. Hong Kong can boast, amongst its trees, of two maples and a small tree of great beauty when in flower *(Pentaphylax euryoides)*, having crowded white blossoms like *Eurya japonica*, which is also found here. The island has also several species of *Euonymus*, a very handsome *Aquilaria* having its flowers in short terminal racemes. *Scolopia chinensis*, a tree allied to that which produces arnatto, is very common in the island; as well as *Schoepfia chinensis*, with axillary racemes of sweet-scented pink flowers.

The coast flora of the island is of the usual tropical marine kind, such as is found on all the islands of the Indian Archipelago right down to Australia. This means mangroves, *Hibiscus tiliaceus, Scævola kænigii, Guilandina bonducella, Acanthus ilicifolius, Morinda, Randia, Vitex,* &c.

FAUNA.—The fauna of Hong Kong includes but a few bats, rodents, birds, and reptiles. A monkey has been seen upon one of the neighbouring islands, and probably, when the population was less, used to visit Hong Kong. It is a short-tailed macacus (*M. St. Johannis*, Swinhoe). I take the following summary from the writings of Mr. Swinhoe in the 'Zoological Proceedings' and the 'Ibis' on the Zoology of China, and the summary of observations on the same subject contained in Dr. Denny's work on the Treaty Ports:—

There is a fair number of species of Chiroptera or bats, a flying fox, *Cynonycteris amplexicaudata*, Geoff., a house-bat, *Vesperugo abramus*, Temm. Also, *V. molossus*, Temm.; *Scotophilus heathii*, Horsf.; *S. temminckii*, Hors.; and *S. pumiloides*, Tom., and several others. The musk-rat (*Sorex murinus, L*), scatters its oppressive perfume as plentifully about the basements of buildings as it does throughout the whole of the East. I have more than once had unpleasant experience of the fact that these animals passing over bottles even with metal capsules, will impart a musky flavour to the contents. A badger (*Meles chinensis*, Gray), common enough in China, has been found in the island, as well as the pale red Chinese fox (*Vulpes hoole*). The Siberian red stoat (*Putorius sibericus*), is a great enemy of the henwife in some villages. A civet (*Vivera zibetha*, Linn.), and a squirrel (*Sciurus castanoventris*, Gray), both widely-spread species, occur on the island, besides rats and mice. The wild boar (*Sus leucomystax*, Temm. and Schl.), affords occasional sport as it does throughout Japan and Central China. There is some talk about a deer (*Cervulus reevesii*, Ogil.).

GEOLOGY.—The island of Hong Kong mainly consists of granite; but there are places where the mica is replaced by hornblende and various changes are undergone by the micas and felspars. In fact it is a most varied rock, besides being penetrated by porphyritic dykes, as well as some of very recent basaltic trap. Excellent instances of the latter can be seen at Quarry Bay. The granite is also somewhat rich in molybdenum. On the shores all round the island excellent sections can be seen, especially from West Point to the north of Stanley, where there are outcrops of granites and metamorphic rocks. At Pok-fa-lum, at the reservoir, the granite assumes a porphyritic character, of dark colour. A similar outcrop is noticed at Deep Bay. Limestone is found in small quantities with large deposits of kaolin, derived from the disintegration of granite rocks. The geology of the island has, however, been well studied, and needs no further notice here.

This concludes my observations on the first part of my travels. In a subsequent portion I shall deal with the Philippine Islands, and some other parts of the south Chinese coast with its dependent islands.

www.ingramcontent.com/pod-product-compliance
Lightning Source LLC
Chambersburg PA
CBHW032239080426
42735CB00008B/917